The *heartbeat* of Hope

31 DAYS FOR
ADVENT
FOR SMALL GROUP
OR PERSONAL USE

The *heartbeat* of Hope

CWR

Elizabeth Rundle

Published 2013 by CWR, Waverley Abbey House, Waverley Lane, Farnham, Surrey GU9 8EP, UK. Registered Charity No. 294387. Registered Limited Company No. 1990308.

For list of National Distributors see www.cwr.org.uk/distributors

Concept development, editing, design and production by CWR

Cover image: fotosearch

Printed in the UK by Page Bros, Norwich

ISBN: 978-1-85345-996-2

Contents

Introduction

'Hope is sparked when something of eternity bursts into our fragile lives. For a moment we lift our eyes from the problems of the world and glimpse things as they could be ... as they will be.' (Andy Frost: Share Jesus International)

Journeying together during these thirty-one days of Advent study, my prayer is that we may all find something of eternity that touches our hearts and deepens our faith. However, I realise Advent is possibly the hardest time of year to 'lift our eyes from the problems', especially when those problems are compounded by the global frenzy to be happy. It's so easy to be overtaken by the avalanche of commercial pressure and material expectations, and, no matter who we are, or where we live, we are not immune from the tensions, fears, regrets, hopes and dreams of the world in which we live.

These human realities of suffering and tragedy confront us in our world, within our communities, our families and even in our own hearts. And, surrounded as we are by piped, seasonal musak, jolly lights, tempting treats and 'To Do' lists of Olympic proportions, an Advent study could seem a step too far. However, this is a special time for disciples of Jesus Christ to listen for the angels' song: 'Glory to God in the Highest and on earth – peace ...' The song is still sung and still heard; the song of universal longing for peace and joy, for love and reconciliation … the age-old hope for things to be as they could be … as they will be.

Let me invite you to explore the pulse of longing for God's Messiah, this heartbeat of hope throughout the Old Testament. Isn't it so exciting to recognise that these are the same hopes that Jesus, as a young boy in the Nazareth synagogue, heard, memorised and shared? As we study, we join our faith with the people of God who, over more than three millennia, have lived and longed for the world as it could be ... God's kingdom of reconciliation, justice and peace.

Tracing the heartbeat of hope we find that hope and trust are often interchangeable in Hebrew scripture. Our journey through Advent helps us to focus our thoughts on our own approach to these words in the light of early Christian experience. You are invited to bring to God your own hopes and fears, and to put all your trust in Him.

Over the years my faith has been enriched by the words of countless people, known and unknown. One of them has been Lord Harries of Pentregarth through his radio contributions. Allow me to share with you his thoughts on Advent: 'Advent is a time of expectation, of hope, and how much we need hope at the moment. Human hopes have so often been dashed to the ground or twisted. Yet hope, like cheerfulness, keeps breaking in.'

The ancient writer of Proverbs noted: 'a cheerful heart makes a cheerful face' – so, in the awesome knowledge that we are loved, accepted and held in the eternal arms of a loving heavenly Father, let's enter into this unique period, this season of gifts and rejoicing, with cheerful, hopeful hearts.

Suggestions for preparation

Maybe you would like to create your own Advent wreath – a circle of evergreen with four candles or tea-lights (one for each week) and a central candle for Christmas Day. Try red or purple for the four weekly candles to represent hope, peace, love and joy: traditionally, the centre candle, which represents Christ the Light of the World, is white. The act of lighting the candle and repeating a 'stilling prayer' becomes a natural and calm beginning to each study. If you are studying as a group, I would also suggest a few moments of personal reflection before moving on to the Bible reading.

Perhaps you could place twenty-five stones or pebbles in a mound on a tray or small table. At one end you place a white candle and at the other a figure to represent yourself. Each day, take away a stone or pebble so that on Christmas Day all 'barriers' have been removed, the rough place will be smooth and the figure can move unhindered to the white candle, the symbol of Emmanuel – God with us in the living presence of Jesus our Lord.

You may like to simply light one candle as a focus for prayer or have a few minutes of a favourite CD to adjust your mind from the day's routine and distractions.

At the end of each week, you will find suggestions for group study.

WEEK 1

Hope in God's Promises

1 DEC

Opening prayer

Calm me, Lord.
May Your Holy Spirit guide me to focus on Your Word.
Centre me into Your deep stillness.

Bible verses

Deuteronomy 18:15–19
Acts 3:18–22

In the book of Deuteronomy we detect the first spark of Messianic hope; the first notes of a recurring song of expectation on which prophets of later centuries would elaborate. Moses was the people's great redeemer; he led them out of slavery in Egypt, delivered the commandments from the Lord God, and trailed the desert places while, over the course of forty years, the former slaves coalesced into a nation. And, of course, the people griped and criticised, they rebelled and looked back on their past life with exaggerated nostalgia, the occupational hazard for every leader in any generation anywhere in the world!

Now fast forward into the New Testament. Our Lord Jesus has been crucified and His dead body sealed in a tomb. After three days He appeared to His disciples. The apostle Paul recorded that over five hundred men and women witnessed the risen Jesus (1 Corinthians 15:6). Before Jesus finally left the earth in physical form, He promised His followers that they would receive the power of the Holy Spirit and be His witnesses from Jerusalem to the ends of the earth (Acts 1:8).

In the holiest of all places, the Temple in Jerusalem, Peter proclaims that Jesus was, and is, the promised Christ (Messiah) and he used the ancient prophecy of Moses to argue his case. To us, we hardly recognise it as a messianic prophecy, but to Peter's audience, it was as well-known as those of Isaiah and Micah. Peter's message shook the listening crowds, yet, in essence it was exactly the same message as the old prophets had uttered; return to God and repent (Acts 3:19–22). Peter was not the only spokesman in the city. Stephen addressed the Sanhedrin, also reminding the learned men of Moses' ancient prophecy. In fact, if you have an odd half an hour, the seventh chapter of Acts is in itself a mini epic, a tour de force of the nation's history. Such was the embedded hope that God would raise up a great prophet, one who would redeem the people and bring about a new order of peace and prosperity, justice and compassion, that every word of prophecy had been cherished through the generations. The men and women who witnessed Jesus' resurrection had no doubts. Jesus was God's promised Messiah.

Think for a moment about the terrain in which Moses and the people of Israel wandered. It's easy to see why God is called 'Rock' so many times in the book of Deuteronomy and in the Psalms. 'Rock' carries all the inference of safety, changelessness, strength and foundation, definitions which carry on in our own thoughts. During this Advent season, we seek to build our lives on Jesus, the promised Holy One of God, our firm and true foundation. This is not an idle wish but a joyous hope as we put our trust in Christ our Lord.

Questions to consider

1. In 1 Timothy 6:17, Paul urges Timothy to command the people to put their hope in God. What are your immediate hopes?
2. Is there a 'Rock' in your life?

Verse

'You are my rock in times of trouble,
You lift me up when I fall down;
All through the storm your love is the anchor,
My hope is in You alone.'

Brian Doerksen

Prayer

Lord Jesus Christ, my Rock and my Redeemer, in these next days, help me to put the miracle of Your coming to earth at the centre of all my preparations.

2 DEC

Opening prayer

Calm me, Lord.
May Your Holy Spirit guide me to focus on Your Word.
Centre me into Your deep stillness.

Bible verses

Jeremiah 33:14–16
Micah 6:6–8

Today we look at challenging messages from God through two very different prophets. Putting these verses together underpins the thought processes of the period, in that the promised Messiah would turn the world from wickedness to justice. The word of the Lord through Micah spells out our responsibility. Biblical literature reverberates with visions of justice, mercy and, that old-fashioned word, righteousness.

As we read these lofty ideals we realise that they were born out of personal and national suffering. Say the name 'Jeremiah' and faces fall at the thought of great tracts of 'Thus saith the Lord!' with long, gloomy prophecies of destruction and woe. However, Jeremiah's written warnings form one of the longest books in the Old Testament. Already, in chapter 31, the Lord God has promised a time will come when everyone will 'know' Him in their hearts. Here in chapter 33 we discover the exciting link between King David and the coming Messiah. As we unravel all the poetic language of roots and branches, the messianic meaning is straightforward. The nature of God's Son (the branch) will be just and righteous. Let's pause for a moment and turn to some words of our Lord Jesus recorded in John 15:5: 'I am the vine; you are the branches'. These words are a clear indication that Jesus saw Himself in a unique relationship with His father God. It was a relationship above and beyond any human relationship, for Jesus said, 'Before Abraham was born, I am' (John 8:58).

Our Advent study is more concerned with the Messianic promises and their fulfilment in our Lord Jesus rather than His specific 'I am' sayings, but to ignore them is to miss a further layer of meaning. We have to look back into the book of Exodus chapter 3 to find the origin and significance of 'I am'. Moses, in his conversation with God, needed to have a name to give to Pharaoh. God told Moses, 'I am'. This is further confirmation that Jesus spoke with God's authority.

Before we turn to Micah, look again at the poignant phrase, 'Jerusalem will live in safety' (Jer. 33:16). For three millennia people have prayed for the peace of Jerusalem and our prayers are still needed in current Middle East politics.

In one of Agatha Christie's Miss Marple stories, Jane Marple explains that although she lives a sheltered life in a village, sooner or later, every aspect of human nature is exposed! Micah came from a little village some twenty or so miles from Jerusalem and prophesied about a century before Jeremiah. His small book is a beautiful example of Hebrew poetry. He was a prophet who looked aghast at the witchcraft, idolatry, violence and widespread dishonesty.

Micah thundered the Lord God's response. The remedy for the people's sin appeared disarmingly simple. It still is. It's not rocket science. It doesn't need years of study. God's remedy for the world's turmoil remains the same as in the days of Micah, and if we could follow that advice, we would draw a little nearer to the kingdom of heaven.

Questions to consider

1. The prophets uttered God's message in visual, dramatic and memorable format. How would you like to see the message of Jesus Christ conveyed beyond church buildings?
2. How can Christians today fight for justice?

Verse

Blessed is He who comes in the name of the Lord,
Blessed indeed is the Lord's Anointed –
Blessed is He, the prophesied, long-awaited Messiah.
His reign will bring true Righteousness,
true Mercy and Peace.
He is the hope of all nations.

Prayer

Dear God, give me a heart for Your justice and mercy.

3 DEC

Opening prayer

Calm me, Lord.
May Your Holy Spirit guide me to focus on Your Word.
Centre me into Your deep stillness.

Bible verses

Isaiah 9:2,6–7
Luke 1:30–33

Pete returned home from two weeks in hospital. A neighbour popped in to see how he was getting on and was delighted to see how well Pete looked. 'I feel fine', said Pete, 'I haven't seen the news for a fortnight!' Whether or not that story is true, I think we can all agree how depressing the news can be at times. Natural disasters, wars, violence on our streets, tragedies of every kind – we see no reason and no end. I look at the television screen and cry for the innocent suffering. But all my sympathies cannot touch the depth of despair felt by those living through the destruction of their homes and livelihoods, the loss of family members and deprivation of all they have ever known. Too many people, while you are reading this, will be going through a dark night of the soul.

And if we can feel discouraged looking at disasters from a distance, it may help us to understand the mind-set of those people who first heard Isaiah's prophecy. They were traumatised. Assyria had invaded the northern kingdom of Israel and deported the useful layer of society. It doesn't take much imagination to realise the Assyrians didn't just offer free camel rides to the conquered Israelites. Their army would have gone in to smash, demoralise and murder any resisters. God's people found themselves in a foreign country, deprived of any means to worship, stripped of all human worth and hope. Physically, economically and spiritually they had reached rock bottom.

Neighbouring Judah awaited a similar fate. It must have seemed a very dark night of the soul.

Isaiah's expansive and stirring prophecy gave hope to the hopeless. Perhaps God would give them a king who would destroy all their enemies and govern with justice and righteousness for ever and ever ... but, wait a moment ... Prince of *Peace*? The people wanted a conquering hero, a more glorious and dominant king than David.

Then, as now, our wish lists do not necessarily coincide with God's purpose. Through the prophet Isaiah, God promised the child would become an all-powerful, compassionate and everlasting Ruler. Names in that culture were of paramount importance because they indicated the true nature of the person, and, one of those names, or titles, would have made the first hearers reel in a double-take. Their first thought on hearing, 'Mighty God' would be the Commandment, 'You shall have no other gods before me' (Exod. 20:3). Did this mean that God himself would be their Redeemer? Was there light at the end of their tunnel?

At the beginning of creation, 'God said, "Let there be light", and there was light' (Gen. 1:3). The Creator God has the power to bring light. Compare this to the words which our Lord Jesus spoke in the seat of religious power, the Temple in Jerusalem: 'I am the light of the world. Whoever follows me will never walk in darkness but will have the light of life' (John 8:12). Jesus is the Redeemer of whom Isaiah prophesied; Jesus is our Mighty God and light in our darkness.

Next time you see twinkling Christmas lights, in a window, draped all over a house, dazzling in a shopping mall or the stars shining on a clear night, thank God for the light He has given into your life. It is a light that no darkness of the soul can extinguish.

Questions to consider

1. In what ways does the birth of a baby herald a new beginning?
2. Which is your favourite title for Jesus?

Verse

Jesus brings His peace and justice,
Heaven's angels 'Glory!' sing;
Hallelujah! Born to save us
Love incarnate, Lord and King.

Prayer

Lord, I praise and thank You for the miracle of each new life.

4 DEC

Opening prayer

Calm me, Lord.
May Your Holy Spirit guide me to focus on Your Word.
Centre me, Lord, into Your deep stillness.

Bible verses

Haggai 1:5–9
Haggai 2:4–7
Haggai 2:20–23

The Old Testament books are crammed with fascinating psychological studies. They lay bare the rainbow of human behaviour which remains prevalent in every community in our own time. Recently, we have become so hooked on the study of human behaviour that a score of TV reality programmes and hundreds of 'How to ...' books for self-advancement bombard our leisure. Popular magazines often include a light-hearted questionnaire by which we are supposed to deduce our own personality, strengths and weaknesses. Strengths give us an immediate lift and good feeling but it's too easy to dismiss judgments of our weaknesses as totally inaccurate. How much easier to focus on the faults of others! Think for a few moments about those with whom you work on a daily basis. You know the people whose encouragement and optimism brings out the best in you and those whose snide criticism, bullying and negative behaviour casts a gloom over your life.

The Bible reading today is taken from a small book of only two chapters. In fact, there are less than forty verses in all and we know next to nothing about the prophet himself. But never mind what we don't know; it's in what we do know that God can speak to us.

We must not forget the importance of names in biblical thought; the name Haggai came from a Hebrew root meaning 'to make pilgrimage'. We could speculate that Haggai had been in captivity with the exiles in Babylon. When Babylon fell to Darius, King of Persia (modern Iran), the exiles were allowed to return to their homeland. However, their joy in repatriation was overshadowed by finding the holy Temple in ruins. The Temple signified the presence of God and a ruined Temple led them to believe that God may have abandoned them. The people soon lost heart in the huge task of rebuilding the Temple and turned their energies into rebuilding their own homes and lives.

Into this scenario steps God's man Haggai. Inspired by the Lord God, he challenges the people to think about their priorities and delivers two wonderful prophecies of hope. First, God's Spirit is with them. They do not need to feel abandoned or afraid, for 'what is desired [Messiah] by all nations will come' (Hag. 2:7). And finally there is the promise that Zerubbabel, from the line of David, will be like God's own 'signet ring' (Hag. 2:23).

Hebrew prophecy and poetry is in every way foreign to our lives and thinking. But when we delve into the ancient thought processes, the message begins to fall into place. The idea of the signet ring was like saying that God guarantees His Messiah will come from Zerubbabel's descendants (Matt. 1:13–16). Do those beautiful words: 'I have chosen you' (Hag. 2:23) remind you of

Jesus' words 'I chose you' in John 15:16?

Haggai's biog is lost in the mists of time, but God in Jesus Christ is present with us now. We don't need to feel impotent in the face of opposition; we need only to claim God's Holy Spirit with us, the same Holy Spirit that was with Haggai. Putting God first puts everything else into perspective.

Questions to consider

1. The people believed God's presence was in the Temple. Is there a particular place where you feel the presence of God more than any other?
2. Are there people you need to encourage today?

Verse

'Your mercy will not fail us, nor leave your work undone;
With your right hand to help us, the victory shall be won.
And then, by all creation your name shall be adored,
And this shall be our anthem:
One church, one faith, one Lord.'

Edward Hayes Plumptre (1821–1891)

Prayer

Loving heavenly Father, keep me rooted and grounded in my Saviour's love.

5 DEC

Opening prayer

Calm me, Lord.
May Your Holy Spirit guide me to focus on Your Word.
Centre me into Your deep stillness.

Bible verses

Isaiah 7:10–14
Matthew 1:18–23

Thomas Beckett was appointed Archbishop of Canterbury in the twelfth century. He took his responsibilities with extreme seriousness. He turned his back on privilege, slept on the floor and gave his rich food to the poor. He dared to disagree with his former friend and mentor, King Henry II. Thomas did not approve of the king's lifestyle or the laws he passed and the king flew into a rage. Tradition has it that Henry shouted out, 'Will no one rid me of this turbulent priest?'

Like Thomas Beckett, Isaiah was brought up in an aristocratic home, he was not afraid of any king and, in a ministry spanning nearly half a century, he relentlessly harried five kings with words from the Lord God of Abraham. I can imagine there were many times when kings and people wanted to see the back of Isaiah. But God's message was not all judgment; there was comfort and hope as well.

Living some seven centuries before the birth of our Lord Jesus, Isaiah is regarded as one of the greatest prophets. He fearlessly proclaimed God's message to repent and be restored into a covenant relationship with God. The political and spiritual situation of Isaiah's time was perilous. Israel and Judah were small, vulnerable nations surrounded by neighbours who worshipped every conceivable god. The people of Israel and Judah on the other hand, worshipped *one* God (Exod. 20:2–3). Both the northern kingdom of Israel and the southern kingdom of Judah heard the words of divine judgment from Isaiah's scathing tongue, but the acid descriptions of their behaviour fell on deaf ears. Rampant injustice and corruption made the rift between the rich and the poor ever wider.

Let's take a backward time-leap and see Isaiah standing before King Ahaz. Regardless of the greatest luxury of the day, the king's court lived in fear of an unholy alliance between the northern neighbours Israel and Syria. The worried king (and previous verses recount that his heart shook), listens to Isaiah, and the prophecy of that day has become pivotal among the messianic hopes. God's divine promise has echoed down through the centuries and around the world. In the New Testament, Matthew repeats this prophecy: '... they will call him Immanuel' adding the explanation, 'which means, "God with us"' (Matt. 1:23). Matthew the Jew, writing for Jewish readers, demonstrates his conviction that Jesus, his Lord and Master, is God's promised Messiah.

How can we fully grasp this astounding truth? The God who sees the world's sin does not abandon His people, but offers them redemption, salvation – He offers them Himself. Desmond Tutu wrote: 'God says: "I am Immanuel, I am God-with-you. I am one who's not going to give you good advice from a safe distance. I enter the fiery furnace with you"'.

The message of Advent calls to us loud and clear. There is no nation or power that can save us. Our sovereign, holy God is with us in the mystery of His son, Jesus Christ.

Questions to consider

1. Are we ever guilty of wanting 'signs' from God before we are prepared to trust Him?
2. There are many forms of idolatry. Make a list of the things that draw people away from God.

Verse

'O come to us, abide with us, Our Lord, Immanuel.'

Phillips Brookes (1835–1893)

Prayer

Lord, You reach out to the world in its deepest, darkest hopelessness.
Through the shadows of my own anxiety,
The dark doubts of night,
I grasp at Your promise: 'I am with you always'.
I whisper the words till they become my peace.

Jill Baker, President of Methodist Women in Britain 2011–2013

6 DEC

Opening prayer

Calm me, Lord.
May Your Holy Spirit guide me to focus on Your Word.
Centre me into Your deep stillness.

Bible verses

Proverbs 8:22–31
John 1:1–14

Last year I heard a really good definition for the words 'wisdom' and 'knowledge'. Knowledge is knowing that a tomato is a fruit. Wisdom is not putting it in the fruit salad.

Alongside the Law and the Prophets, the Hebrew Bible revered the wisdom literature, of which the book of Proverbs is a part. Some combine truth and humour, as in: 'A foolish son is his father's ruin and a quarrelsome wife is like a constant dripping' (19:13)! These wise sayings, in the pithy format of Hebrew poetry, are easy to remember. Our particular section for today offers a wider dimension to the nature of God.

So many names were attributed to Israel's God: the Lord God of Hosts, Almighty God, the Most High, Immanuel, and Sovereign Lord to name a few, but in Proverbs we find that God is 'wisdom'. As with so much ancient, cross-cultural, translated language, we lose much of the original power and nuance of such words. Wisdom, in the time of King Solomon, held together concepts of reason, the fundamental meaning of things, and purpose. The whole of chapter 8 rings with the call of wisdom, a call that would have been familiar to Jesus, to the gospel writer, John, and to his first audience. Wisdom was before and part of creation itself. In the enigmatic book of Job, chapter 28 is devoted to finding wisdom. Job cries, 'Where can wisdom be found?' (v.12) and the answer is, 'God ... alone knows where it dwells' (v.23). So wisdom becomes an integral part of God's nature.

Proverbs are poetic spiritual truths, giving us insight into the life of Old Testament times and the constant call of God to turn to Him and, in response to His loving care, live good, sensible and productive lives. The combination of deity with wisdom lingered into the Christian era. Remember that vivid account of Mary and Joseph's frantic search for the twelve-year-old Jesus? Luke throws in the pointed phrase: 'And Jesus grew in wisdom ...' (Luke 2:52).

However, the prologue of John's Gospel pulls the threads of mystery into the person of Jesus. The Greek word for 'word' in those opening verses had its roots 600 years BC. It came to mean the creative force, the expression of God and in the Aramaic of Jesus' day, 'word' meant divine wisdom. All these meanings used to impart a stupendous truth that the Word, the reason, the fundamental meaning and purpose of God is to bring light to everyone's life. Yet the truth of this divine action blazes afresh to each generation and the miracle is, of all the horrendous evil and darkness that the world has known since the coming of Jesus, that His light has never been extinguished.

At the beginning of his letter to the first Christians in Corinth, Paul argues that Jesus Christ is the wisdom and the power of God (1 Cor. 1–2). These themes connect us to the very first disciples who struggled to make sense of the world's negative and violent response. All these centuries later we can rejoice in:

- the universal sovereignty of God in Jesus Christ
- His intimate care and relationship with believers right in the middle of their own situations
- the continuing challenge to bring the light of Christ into the world's darkness and live to make the world a better place.

Questions to consider

1. Which Proverb is your favourite and why?
2. Where would you look to find divine wisdom?

Verse

'O Word of God incarnate,
O Wisdom from on high,
O Truth unchanged, unchanging,
O Light of our dark sky.'

W.W. How (1823–1897)

Prayer

Lord, be the strength for my weakness, the wisdom for my foolishness and the light that guides me now and always.

7 DEC

Opening prayer

Calm me, Lord.
May Your Holy Spirit guide me to focus on Your Word.
Centre me into Your deep stillness.

Bible verses

Ezekiel 34:15–24
John 10:10–11

Over the past decade Street Pastors have become an interdenominational witness in over a hundred and fifty British towns and cities. This ministry is creeping internationally, with Street Pastors now operating in the Channel Isles, Antigua and a northern suburb of Sydney, Australia. To quote the writer of ancient wisdom: '... what has been done will be done again; there is nothing new under the sun' (Eccl. 1:9) and I suggest we can claim Ezekiel as an original Street Pastor. Not that Ezekiel sat down with drunken girls or dispensed flip-flops and bottles of water, but he was the voice of religious conscience of his time and took God's message into the streets. Some of his enacted parables, by today's criteria, would appear way out, but their visual impact ensured that they were memorable! The early chapters of his prophecies are loaded with visions of sin and judgment, doom and gloom. Ezekiel lived through the destruction of Jerusalem and was taken into exile where he preached in the streets of Babylon for twenty-two years.

Whenever we come across overt longing for justice and mercy, peace and security, we know the author writes from an opposite situation. These were brave men. What ridicule and persecution they suffered, but they held on to their faith, hope and trust that, in God's time, things would be different. Ezekiel endured frustration, depression and persecution, but he never lost his trust in God; a day would come when the Lord God himself would intervene and abolish all the oppression and corruption suffered by His sheep (Ezek 34:16). The last fifteen chapters of this influential prophet change gear to offer glorious visions of hope.

The majority of people today have never been within two metres of a sheep and modern shepherds go out to their enormous flocks in 4x4s. The intimate relationship that former shepherds had with their small flocks has all but disappeared. However, it is this shepherd concept we need to fix in our minds if we are to grasp the truth of these passages. The image of a shepherd equals constant care and provision; it is the shepherd who helps the creatures out of a ditch, or lifts them up when they are stuck on their backs. The shepherd guards and protects his sheep, knowing each individual animal – a beautiful image of gentleness without parallel.

Compare the vision of Isaiah 40:11. 'He tends his flock like a shepherd. He gathers the lambs in his arms and carries them close to his heart; he gently leads those that have young.' Sheep are trusting. Sheep will follow. They will also wander off and get into all sorts of tricky situations if left to themselves. Jesus knew all these references to shepherds and sheep were not only directly related to God and His people but also to the leadership role of the Messiah. Now think of what Jesus said of Himself. Our Lord laid specific claim to being the Good Shepherd, the one who would lay down His life for the sheep. These are not mere pastoral ideals or whimsical poetic dreams. These are the words of our Saviour, who, through perfect love and sacrifice, offers us new hope and new life. Can you put your trust in the Good Shepherd to lift you out of danger, carry you in His arms and call your name?

Questions to consider

1. Have there been times when you needed gentleness and protection?
2. Pray for Street Pastors who, tonight, will take the compassion of Jesus to those who have 'lost their way'.

Verse

Jesus my Shepherd, brother, friend,
My prophet, Priest and King,
My Lord, my Life, my way, my end,
Accept the praise I bring.

Charles Wesley (1707–1788)

Prayer

May the God of peace, that great Shepherd of the sheep, equip me for doing His will, through Jesus Christ my Lord, to whom be the glory for ever and ever.

(Based on Hebrews 13:20-21)

Suggestions for group study for Week 1

Preparation

Light the first candle on an Advent wreath and play a CD song or piece of instrumental music to focus the group.

Focus

Choose a day from the week and say the opening prayer. Then consider the Bible readings, inviting as many people as possible to read. After reading the Bible passage, consider the mighty themes of the Bible:

- the universal sovereignty of God
- God's intimate care of and personal relationship with those who put their trust in Him.

Discussion point:

'If God has promised to guide His people (and He has) then if you sincerely want to do His will, He does guide you, even when it doesn't seem like it.'

Cliff Richard

Prayer:

Lord Jesus, as we sing the familiar carols and hear the well-loved readings this Christmas, touch our hearts afresh with the challenge and excitement of Your birth.

Conclude by saying the Lord's Prayer and sharing either the Grace or the Peace.

WEEK 2

Hope in His Unfailing Love

This second week I have called Adagio. The initial impetus slows down. We recognise the time scale of prophecy, the endless years of waiting, the unquenchable hope that kept people looking to God, confident that one day He would send His Messiah to change the world.

8 DEC

Opening prayer

Eternal God, source of all peace,
May Your Holy Spirit guide me to the truths within Your Word.
Centre me into Your deep stillness.

Bible verses

Psalm 33:1–5,20–22
Colossians 3:12–17

Christmas cards are dropping on the mat – it's time to create my 'gallery of friends'. Many cards contain newsy letters and some include photos. My doors become an ideal display area and are my way to remember and pray for friends and family, giving thanks to God for all that each person means. Usually there is one card which I call my favourite. The picture that captured my attention last year was a conventional nativity scene, painted by mouth. I went online to know more about this talented artist and was moved by his deep faith. I discovered that Paulus Ploier had become paralysed at the age of nineteen when he dived head-first into water that was shallower than he expected. Paulus says God showed him what it was to feel and to love. He makes a distinction between *believing* God is there for us and *knowing* God is there for us. Paulus *knows* God is there for him and his art, love and belief are the things that guide his life. To me it is now so much more than a Christmas card – it is a work of love, a living demonstration of Immanuel, God with us in every situation. It speaks to me of great triumph through the heartache of disaster, of the strength we can find in God's unfailing love. Look again at the last three verses of Psalm 33. What a powerful challenge from the word of God – words that would have given strength and hope to the early Christians as they faced persecution.

It's December – let's turn our minds to Mediterranean warmth! The Colossians lived in a fertile valley in present day Turkey. They had enjoyed a vibrant woollen trade with corresponding wealth and influence. But by the time of Paul's letter, the town was in decline: eclipsed by nearby modern cities, Colossae was in the relegation zone. It's an intriguing scenario; one of the smallest letters in the New Testament, written to a fading, insignificant community by a man they had never met! Yet this letter contains some of the most Christ-centred and relevant teaching. You may have heard today's verses from chapter 3 read at a wedding. Clearly they were not intended for that kind of occasion, however they are words that fit comfortably for a wedding or any other service as universal guidelines for every follower of Jesus Christ.

I'd just like to draw your attention to verses 12 and 14. Paul cleverly uses imagery of their woollen industry by writing 'clothe' yourselves and the original word used for 'put on' was the same word we have for 'brooch'. The Greek word for bind is interchangeable with brooch. So we can say we will 'put on' love, a love that clasps us, embraces us and holds us together with God's people. These are inspired words of hope for those who feel marginalised, overtaken by events beyond their control, saddened by fading influence and changing times. If you are tempted to feel like that, remember that Paul wrote those words from prison!

When I look at my own short-comings, short fuse and impatience, I sometimes think it would be a good idea to read these words *every* morning.

Questions to consider

1. How would you describe the birth of Jesus as the fulfilment of God's unfailing love?
2. Art, love and belief guide Paulus Ploier's life. What guides your life?

Verse

'Love came down at Christmas,
Love all lovely, Love Divine.
Love was born at Christmas,
Star and Angels gave the sign.'

Christina Rossetti (1830–1894)

Prayer

I pray to know the Love that will never let me go.

9 DEC

Opening prayer

Eternal God, source of all peace,
May Your Holy Spirit guide me to the truths within Your Word.
Centre me into Your deep stillness.

Bible verses

Ezekiel 37:11
John 11:43–45

International evangelist, Tony Campolo, gave one of his books the intriguing title *20 Hot Potatoes Christians are Afraid to Touch*. Perhaps there are several areas you find difficult especially when life seems to treat some people so unfairly. Julie and her husband had hoped for a big family. After being married for several years, they invested in IVF treatment and, to their utter joy, Julie gave birth to twin girls. However, soon after the birth she was diagnosed with cancer. Months of treatment followed, but sadly, Julie died. The twins were three years old. The family was devastated; all their prayers for a cure for the cancer had come to nothing – their hearts were broken.

Tragic though this family situation was, they were by no means the only family suffering grief amid the media hype to 'Have a Happy Christmas'. We do not understand these things, and there are no pat answers of comfort. We can only be there, walk with them through the valley of the shadow of death, assure them of our love and support and maybe offer some practical help. It is totally understandable to feel that all hope is gone.

In our Bible reading, the prophet Ezekiel addressed the exiled community with a vision of new life. I'm sure most of them would have laughed in his face. After all, they were hundreds of miles from everything they knew and loved; their spirits were broken; their hope had gone. But the Lord gave Ezekiel that inspiring promise.

God will raise them from the death of exile and renew their life by his Spirit. The promise of resurrection!

As the vision of life into dry bones epitomised God's power over life and death, we find that same power demonstrated by our Lord Jesus in the raising of Lazarus. We are not asked to understand, just to trust.

In 1865 a young man rode his horse the six miles from Jerusalem into Bethlehem. So inspirational was his journey and the sight of the little hill-top town with the vast mountains of Moab in the background, that he was inspired to write a Christmas carol. He wrote it initially for the children at his church, but it has struck a chord all over the world with young and old to become one of the best-loved carols of all. A verse, which no longer appears in hymn books, ends with the lines:

'Where love stands watching and faith holds wide the door,
The dark night wakes, the glory breaks,
And Christmas comes once more.'

Phillips Brooks, the author of the famous carol, *O little town of Bethlehem*, became a celebrated preacher and Bishop of Massachusetts. He stood with many a parishioner in their bleak moments and gave to them his utter trust in the life to come, prepared for us in the presence of God.

Questions to consider

1. Is there a sad situation for which you need to pray today?
2. Which passage of Scripture do you turn to when you need hope?

Verse

'Breathe on me, breath of God,
Fill me with life anew,
That I may love what Thou dost love,
And do what Thou wouldst do.

Breathe on me, breath of God,
So shall I never die,
But live with Thee the perfect life
Of Thine eternity.'

Edwin Hatch (1835–1889)

Prayer

Lord, I pray for the renewing power of Your Holy Spirit, that I may know the comfort of Your unfailing love.

10 DEC

Opening prayer

Eternal God, source of all peace,
May Your Holy Spirit guide me to the truths within Your Word.
Centre me into Your deep stillness.

Bible verses

Micah 4:1–4
Micah 5:2,4–5a
John 14:27

On 10 December 1964, Rev Dr Martin Luther King was awarded the Nobel Prize for Peace; a global recognition of his non-violent stand against segregation and humiliation imposed on his fellow Americans of African and Caribbean origin. Peace – that illusory dream, the hope that beats in the heart of 99.9 per cent of the world's population. Walk into any home or shop in Bethlehem and hear the greeting, 'Salaam'. Walk into any home or shop in Jerusalem and hear the same greeting, 'Shalom'. This word 'peace' is voiced in the Holy Land, the land crippled with division, toxic mistrust and history of blame, more than anywhere else on the planet. How poignant then is the ancient prophet's word picture of a world where no one will be afraid and wars will cease. Once more we unravel the intricacies of language. We pray for peace when confronted by the tragic waste and violence of war. We use one small word to mean absence from conflict. The biblical meaning embraces far more. It signifies wholeness, safety, completeness, health, harmony, tranquillity and a state free from agitation. Shalom is a greeting of mighty blessings on several levels that come together in one word. The apostle Paul wrote (Phil. 4:7) that the peace of God transcends all our human understanding.

One September afternoon, inside a pilgrim coach parked near the separation wall in Bethlehem, those ancient words of the prophet Micah brought tears to my eyes (Micah 5:5a). God's promised ruler, the Messiah, was to be the people's peace. There could hardly be a more stark contradiction between the hope and the reality. But let us look at what our Lord Jesus said: '... my peace I give you' (John 14:27). Can we take that in? Our Saviour reaches out in the power of the Holy Spirit to give us mighty blessings, to keep us free from agitation, to bring harmony within relationships, a healing and wholeness we can never find in the world. What a promise – what a gift!

We met Micah on 2 December. His prophecies berated the breakdown of society in Judah; his passionate oratory alternated between God's anger and judgment to God's promise of forgiveness and restoration. It is a book of contrasts powerfully evoking God's authority alongside His everlasting love. Micah lived through the reign of three kings and his words reveal that over that period, things did not improve! However, for us on our Advent journey, this is the first thrilling mention of Bethlehem as the place from which God's Ruler, the long-awaited Messiah, would come. And notice that we have the shepherd concept featured once more! How interesting to see the culmination of this short but great prophecy is none other than the hope of God's peace.

Questions to consider

1. Whom would you like to nominate for a Nobel Peace Prize?
2. Can you think of anything better than peace?

Verse

> 'How beautiful on the mountains are the feet of those who bring good news,
> Who proclaim peace, who bring good tidings,
> Who proclaim salvation, who say to Zion:
> "Your God reigns!"
> How beautiful when all the ends of the earth will see the salvation of our God.'
>
> Poetry from the great prophet Isaiah

Prayer

I join my prayers with millions who long for peace. I pray for those whose lives have been ruined by war, those who are too frightened to sleep for fear of violence. I pray for those who have no peace of mind. Lord, I pray for Your blessing of shalom.

11 DEC

Opening prayer

Eternal God, source of all peace,
May Your Holy Spirit guide me to the truths within Your Word.
Centre me in Your deep stillness.

Bible verses

Psalm 117
Galatians 3:26–29

It's enriching when members of the congregation are willing to read Bible passages in worship. However, if I ask someone to read Psalm 117 (the *whole* of it), I must admit to the fun of seeing the designated reader's initial panic. Amusement is shared when the reader recognises that, with only two verses, it is the shortest Psalm of all!

Short it may be, but what a dynamic profession of faith! The psalmist takes a huge and uncharacteristic leap beyond the usual narrow horizon. 'Praise the LORD, *all* [my emphasis] you nations', an extraordinary glimpse of God's inclusive love. Another millennium would pass before the Apostle Paul would quote from this Psalm in his letter to the first Christians in Rome (Rom. 15:11).

Some of the Old Testament writings have an unfortunate dual aspect. On one hand the writer prays for blessings on the righteous then, in the same breath, demands that God obliterate evil-doers with all power and vengeance! These are similar thought patterns of reward and punishment to the current promises of Father Christmas bringing toys to good children while naughty children won't receive any presents.

Our small Psalm is a mighty banner of hope. There will be a time, God's time, when enmity and fighting will cease. All nations, in other words Jews and Gentiles, will praise the Lord together. The whole world will acknowledge the faithful love of the Creator of our intricate and mesmerisingly fabulous world. We find this underlined in the words of our Lord Jesus: 'For God so loved the world, that he gave his one and only Son, that whoever believes in him shall not perish but have eternal life' (John 3:16). Jesus gave a reason, a fact and a consequence. There is nothing exclusive with God; His love is available for all people and Paul is eager to promote our unity in Jesus Christ (Gal. 3:28).

Visiting the Holy Land is a vivid reminder of this inclusive love. Pilgrims from Australia to Zimbabwe, Italy to India, stream through the holy sites, a tidal-wave of ethnic costumes, different languages and skin tones. It is indeed a heart-warming foretaste of the kingdom of God. And along the pilgrim route, various plaques challenge the passer-by with food for thought. A plaque in Bethany reads: 'Today as in the past, the love of Jesus seeks a refuge where he is lovingly expected and where he can rest. He finds our hearts are filled with distractions – he longs for us to empty our hearts and lovingly receive him'.

Together with Psalm 117 and Paul's words from Galatians, those words speak to me as I scurry about with all the preparations for Christmas. They centre my thoughts on the reason, the fact and consequence of Christ's birth. Don't let's be distracted from our praise and worship.

Questions to consider

1. Are there ways in which you would like to see people of different faiths coming together in your community?
2. If you have had a particularly bad day, list the ways in which, with hindsight, you can see still God's faithfulness and love.

Verse

Sow Hope in the furrows of darkness,
Water the seed with your love;
Embrace in your prayers those who don't sing your songs,
God's bounty and faithfulness prove.
Live in the moment with Hope in your heart
See – the world is a wonderful place;
Hold hands with each nation to praise our Creator,
The God of all Truth and all Grace.

Prayer

Lord, I pray for .... (name children you know)
May they be guided to know the difference between a fairy story and what is the most wonderful, life-changing story in the world.
May Jesus become real in their lives.

12 DEC

Opening prayer

Eternal God, source of all peace,
May Your Holy Spirit guide me to the truths within Your Word.
Centre me into Your deep stillness.

Bible verses

Mark 4:26–29
James 5:5–11

'The bells of waiting Advent ring ...' So begins John Betjeman's much loved poem 'Christmas', often quoted in Advent carol services. Reading it the other day, the word 'bells' caught my imagination and I began to think about all the ringing that goes on in our lives.

Telephones, mobiles, door-bells, the pings and dings of appliances, school bells, the ringing wail of ambulance and police sirens, and the alarm clock that rings all too soon to wake us. And let's not forget church bells! A friend is waiting for a kidney transplant and she has just been fitted with a bleeper, an alarm which might ring at any time to call her for a life-transforming operation. All these bells! A background to our life of calls and alarms, sounds we cannot ignore.

Yet, this line of Betjeman's poem denotes a very different and tranquil setting; an unhurried, rhythmic peel of age-old bells calling people to stop, think and worship. In that tranquil mode the poet writes of 'waiting' Advent. I doubt if many of us are good at waiting. The bombarding adverts would have us believe there is no need to wait. We can have it now. This 'now' culture has us in its grip and removes us from the natural rhythms of our agricultural ancestors – farmers and gardeners have no alternative than to wait, to be patient and to trust in the silent growth.

James, the first leader of the organised church in Jerusalem, wrote: 'See how the farmer waits for the land to yield its valuable crop patiently waiting ... You too, be patient and stand firm, because the Lord's coming is near' (James 5:7–8). This farming parable didn't mean that whilst waiting, the farmer would twiddle his thumbs. Everyone knew that work on the land is ongoing and constant but there is nothing instant about the harvest. Waiting can be hard, especially if, like my friend, you are waiting on news from the doctor or the hospital. Waiting and trusting takes all our reserves of patience and grace.

In the parable of the growing seed, we realise our Lord Jesus was talking about spiritual growth. Our faith needs time to grow quietly, away from the world's clamour. It needs gentle cultivation, the right food. We cannot engineer or hurry faith. As the seed begins to transform from the seed into the stalk and the grain, the Holy Spirit is transforming us. We are in God's hands and in His timing.

We wait to celebrate the coming of the Word of God in the form of a vulnerable baby, but the first Christians were waiting for Christ's coming again in power and glory. As we prepare to celebrate the first coming, let us commit ourselves to live in hope and expectation of the second coming. The words spoken in the Eucharist service are explicit: 'Christ has died. Christ is risen. Christ will come again'.

This is where our human understanding leaves us as it were, at the top of a ski-jump. We can turn back or we can place our hopes and our trust in Jesus and launch out in faith. Millions have done just that and found in Jesus their Saviour and friend.

Questions to consider

1. What do bells mean in your life?
2. Is there someone in a waiting situation for whom you need to pray?

Verse

'All my heart this night rejoices,
As I hear, far and near,
Sweetest angel voices.
Christ is born! The choirs are singing,
Till the air, everywhere
Now with joy is ringing.'

Paul Gerhardt (1607–1676)

Prayer

Lord help me to wait, to listen and to grow in faith.

13 DEC

Opening prayer

Eternal God, source of all peace,
May Your Holy Spirit guide me to the truths within Your Word.
Centre me into Your deep stillness.

Bible verses:

Deuteronomy 8:11–19
1 John 4:7–12

I expect you are thinking 'This doesn't sound very Christmassy', but what exactly is 'Christmassy'? Carol services? Lights and decorations in shops and houses? Songs to remind us that Santa is coming? The annual nativity? Are we expected to suddenly switch on happiness when we switch on the Christmas tree lights? For most of us, the last couple of weeks before Christmas becomes a natural time for looking back and memories flood in with every Christmas card, letter, email and phone call. This is the time to look back not just over our spiritual journey of the past year, but back to the time when the coming of Jesus into the world made an impact on our lives. It is a time to look back and remember those dear people who encouraged and loved us into faith. And we must never forget the millions of lives changed by Jesus Christ and those whose faith in the living Lord has brought, and brings today, persecution and death. We could say that the Old Testament is a compilation of events to show how God intervened in human history, recorded to make sure His people did not forget. Reading the momentous saga of God's guidance and providence for the Children of Israel, we can be tempted to ask: How could they possibly forget?

When we study the Bible we meet people like ourselves; one moment overwhelmed by the presence of God, but with little staying power, we do, as they did, soon forget. This special time of Advent is a great gift. God gives us the gift of looking back – back to the manger where a young mother placed her first baby, safely out of the range of animal hooves ... back to all those stories of Jesus ... back to those early Christian believers to whom Paul the apostle wrote: 'But when the set time had fully come, God sent his Son, born of a woman ...' (Gal. 4:4).

Some will have the excitement of a family gathering, watching children open their presents and generally enjoy a welcome break from routine. It's easy to celebrate when things are going well. But across the road there is probably someone else who cringes with every 'Happy Christmas' greeting. They avoid the loaded shops because they have no one with whom to share Christmas, or they can't afford the extras everyone else seems to be enjoying. Then another segment approaches Christmas with dread at the thought of having to endure the company of certain family members.

Advent brings into sharp focus our humanity, our vulnerability, our joys and our tears. In his pamphlet, *I'm not ashamed*, former Archbishop of Canterbury, Dr George Carey, wrote about his feelings that Christianity was being air-brushed out of Christmas. He said, 'The real meaning of Christmas is the celebration of the powerful story of God breaking through human misery, poverty and sin to be with us.' Yes – that is what we must never forget, each Christmas and each day, that whatever has happened, or whatever we face in the future, God in Jesus Christ is with us in His saving love.

Questions to consider

1. At this special time of year, what and whom do you remember? Have you told them?
2. How do you think biblical characters would regard our forgetfulness of God's presence with us?
3. Do you contrast or merge with the secular celebrations around you?

Verse

'We'll praise Him for all that is past
And trust Him for all that's to come.'

Joseph Hart (1712–1768)

Prayer

Thank You, Lord, for the precious gift of memory.
Thank You for blessing my life with family and friends who have been a shoulder to cry on and in whose company I can be myself.

14 DEC

Opening prayer

Eternal God, source of all peace,
May Your Holy Spirit guide me to the truths within Your Word.
Centre me in Your deep stillness.

Bible verses

Matthew 1:19–25
Mark 2:1–12

Claire's steep learning curve in regard to forgiveness was very personal and painful. Her mother gave birth to her in the days when it was a stigma to be illegitimate. Deep in Claire's heart the resentment festered. She could not forgive her mother. Then, one day, a friend said to her, 'She could have given you away'. Those words hit like a bolt of lightning. The obvious had never occurred to Claire. From that moment she was able to see the sacrifices her mother had made and all the positive things in her upbringing.

Forgiveness released Claire from a heavy, subconscious burden. Advent was, traditionally, a time of repentance, but in the more comfortable message of God's love, peace and joy, this has largely been bypassed. However, the themes of repentance, forgiveness and reconciliation became inextricable with the Messianic prophecies, without diminishing the idea of God as judge. In all the desperate longing for the Messiah to vanquish the oppressors, eliminate the corrupt and herald the kingdom of God, it is easy to pass over one of the fundamental reasons for the Messiah's coming. Matthew confidently states in the early verses of his Gospel that Jesus will 'save his people from their sins' (Matt. 1:21). Human nature is very good at missing the obvious.

Concepts of sacrifice, redemption and sin are pretty alien to our twenty-first century minds. So let's pretend we are back in the first century. All our lives we have been taught that only God is able to forgive sins. We know Isaiah's prophecy about God the suffering Servant who would take upon Himself 'the iniquity of us all' (Isa. 53:6) and we've heard the rumour that when John the Baptist saw Jesus coming towards him for baptism he exclaimed: 'Look, the Lamb of God who takes away the sin of the world!'(John 1:29). Then we get the chance to listen to the Teacher himself. What Jesus says is both shocking and thrilling. Jesus forgives.

One of the best and most profoundly moving ways of confronting the idea of forgiveness was in Her Majesty Queen Elizabeth II's Christmas address of 2011. With dignity and sincerity, she looked directly into the camera lens to say, 'Although we are capable of great acts of kindness, history teaches us that we sometimes need saving from ourselves – from our recklessness or our greed. God sent into the world a unique person ... a Saviour with the power to forgive. Forgiveness lies at the heart of the Christian faith. It can heal broken families, it can restore friendships and it can reconcile divided communities. It is in forgiveness that we feel the power of God's love.'

As Christians in a secular world, as God's faithful remnant, it is our daily challenge to follow our Lord's teaching, and it can be uncomfortable to realise our own need of forgiveness. Praise God in

Jesus Christ that through His sacrifice on the cross we can all find forgiveness and know the saving power of God's love. Is there a corner of your life that needs the touch of your Saviour?

Questions

1. How did it feel when someone forgave you?
2. Can we claim to be followers of Jesus Christ if we remain unforgiving?

Verse

'Come, O long-expected Jesus,
Come and speak your saving word;
From our fears and sins release us,
Hear our prayer: "Forgive us, Lord".

Come, O long-expected Jesus,
Born a child and yet a King,
Born for humankind's salvation,
Justice and forgiveness bring.'

Based on a Charles Wesley Advent hymn

Prayer

Lord, forgive me my many failings. I ask forgiveness for my sins. Forgive me too for the times when I haven't been aware that what I have said or done has hurt others. Help me, guide me and, in Your name, give me grace to be forgiving.

Suggestions for group study for Week 2

Preparation

Light the second candle on an Advent wreath and play a song or piece of instrumental music to focus the group.

Focus

Choose a day from the week and say the opening prayer. Then consider the Bible readings, inviting as many people as possible to read. Refer to the input and questions.

Discussion point

> 'The best way to not feel hopeless is to get up and do something. If you go out and make some good thing happen, you will fill the world with hope and you will fill yourself with hope.'
>
> President Obama

Prayer

> *Lord, Your gift to us of Your very self still lies, unwrapped, in the forgotten corners of the world. Give us, today, the joy of rediscovering Your presence in the presence of each other.*
>
> *(Margaret Silf)*

Conclude by saying the Lord's Prayer and sharing either the Grace or the Peace.

WEEK 3

Be Joyful in Hope

The heartbeat of hope moves up a notch from Adagio to Andante. This slightly quicker pace invites us to walk purposefully with the Word of God and to reflect on how Jesus saw Himself and was interpreted by His disciples in the light of Old Testament scriptures.

15 DEC

Opening prayer

Lord of hopefulness, Lord of all joy,
May Your Holy Spirit open my eyes to the wonder of Your promises.
Still me, Lord, to receive Your blessing.

Bible verses

Isaiah 35:1–6
Luke 1:67–79

Can you imagine what it would be like if you were unable to speak? How could we work without speaking? Speech is an automatic response. In countless languages from all ages, millions of words are uttered every second – whispers to shouts, advice and comfort, information and affection – a never-ending buzz of voices. Zechariah found himself isolated from normal, everyday conversation, locked into silence.

So why should we bother with this peripheral character? How can we discover God's Word to us in this strange outpouring which sounds more Old than New Testament? Let's look at the timeless elements faithfully recorded by Luke: praise, conviction and hope.

Zechariah's first words on recovering his speech were in praise of God. Then follows a total conviction that God's promises are to be fulfilled and a bursting expectation that the eight-day-old son he held in his arms would be the one to prepare the way for the Messiah. Zechariah was educated in all the Law and the Prophets but when the angel appeared to him, he suddenly lost his confidence.

I think we can extend our sympathy to Zechariah; we can all have times when at a particular testing point, our faith shrivels. He had nine months of silence in which to meditate on the angel's words and to search the Scriptures. We can be sure he soaked himself in Scripture because his great song is packed with echoes from the prophets and psalms. We can pick out the themes we've met before: God's promise, salvation from David's lineage, righteousness, forgiveness of sins and peace. And now all this was to come true in the lifetime of Zechariah's son. The promised Messiah was almost a reality.

Notice, as well, that Luke writes, 'Zechariah was filled with the Holy Spirit' (Luke 1:67). Year by year we celebrate the coming of Jesus into our world. We put up jolly lights, send our cards, exchange gifts of love and party. How different for godly Jews like Zechariah – the coming of God's Messiah into the world was a stupendous event which they had awaited for hundreds of years. The song of Zechariah carries the nation's heartbeat of hope – through their darkest hours, the faithful remnant never gave up hope that, one day, God would honour the promise made to Abraham. The Messiah would bring about a new world order of security and prosperity, He would save His people and even the blind and dumb would be able to see and sing. Zechariah was able to proclaim the imminent fulfilment of those prophecies, for his mute tongue gave voice to this song of joy.

The eternal mystery and miracle of Christ's coming was prophesied; He came and still comes to each waiting heart. Zechariah looked forward to a better world and we, in our turn, in the power of the Holy Spirit, can claim the liberating impact of Immanuel, God with us, in the person of Jesus Christ.

Questions to consider

1. What do you find are the greatest barriers to being 'joyful in hope'?
2. What hopes would you like to pass on to future generations?

Verse

'All my hope on God is founded;
Human pride and earthly glory, sword and crown betray our trust;
What with care and toil we fashion, tower and temple fall to dust.
But God's power, hour by hour, is my temple and my tower.'

Based on Joachim Neander (1650–1680)

Prayer

Lord, I pray today for those who have suddenly lost their speech through illness. I pray also for therapists who seek to restore speech and for those whose loved ones can no longer speak to them.

16 DEC

Opening Prayer

Lord of all hopefulness, Lord of all joy.
May Your Holy Spirit open my eyes to the wonder of Your promises.
Still me, Lord, to receive Your blessing.

Bible verses:

2 Corinthians 4:6–9,16–18
Luke 7:11–17

At face value, you might wonder what the widow of Nain and her son have got to do with Messianic prophecies. I can reassure you that, for the gathered crowds around Jesus and for the early readers and audience of Luke's gospel, the link resonated loud and clear. It had been four hundred years since the people had heard the Word of the Lord God through a prophet and the last of those great men was Malachi. The Lord God gave His man in Jerusalem some mighty promises; you can find them in Malachi 4. In essence:

- the Day of the Lord is coming; the reckoning, the judgment and the destruction of all evil
- the sun of righteousness will rise with healing for the faithful; God's Messiah would heal and save
- before that day, God will send the prophet Elijah (Mark 9:5).

And what did Elijah do (1 Kings 17:17–24)? Elijah restored to life the widow's son at Zarephath. The circumstances in which both widows found themselves were the worst possible tragedy. To lose a husband was to lose protection and maintenance, to lose a son was to lose their future hope. Jesus demonstrated God's compassion for those hardest hit by life's disasters and the people responded to Jesus by saying, 'God has come to help his people' (Luke 7:16). In other words, that glorious Immanuel moment – God is with us in Jesus Christ.

In the weeks and days leading to Christmas, the tragedies that occur seem to take on a heightened significance. Back in January 2010, a massive earthquake devastated the Caribbean island of Haiti. Death and devastation tore the heart out of the islanders. One of the main Christian leaders, the president of the Methodist church in Haiti, Rev Gesner Paul, recently wrote a letter of thanks to those who had subscribed to the rebuilding of the island's infra-structure.

'We must face the challenge of working to raise Haiti from the ashes. We have been called to work in a difficult context, but as leaders, we must be the last ones to lose hope. Yes, let us maintain this hope that helps us triumph and believe that rebirth is still possible.'

I believe Jesus expects us to respond with His compassion to the crying needs we see, whether those needs be in a local situation or, as in the case of Haiti, far away. Whatever we do, whether it is to volunteer within a charitable organisation – and there are so many – visit the lonely or cook for those struck down by sudden illness, disability or bereavement, Advent is a time to explore opportunities and prepare for spiritual and practical action in the coming year.

I wonder how many Haitians clung to the words of Paul: 'struck down but not destroyed' (2 Cor. 4:9)? Is Jesus asking you to help someone not lose heart, not lose hope and find new life in Him?

Questions to consider

1. Have you ever been involved with a rebuilding project at home or abroad?
2. Why do we generally expect our leaders to have more hope than most?

Verse

'Hail the heaven-born Prince of Peace,
Hail the Sun of Righteousness!
Light and Life to all he brings,

Risen with healing in his wings.
Mild he lays his glory by, born that man no more may die,
Born to raise the sons of earth,
Born to give them second birth:
Hark, the herald angels sing,
"Glory to the new-born King".'

Charles Wesley (1707–1788)

Prayer

Lord, Jesus Christ, I bring to you my deepest need. I pray for Your healing into the tragedies and sorrows of life. I pray for the assurance that You are with me through all things.

17 DEC

Opening prayer

Lord of all hopefulness, Lord of all joy,
May Your Holy Spirit open our eyes to the wonder of Your promises.
Still me, Lord, to receive Your blessing.

Bible verses

Matthew 3:4–6
Luke 3:1–18

Beethoven's Ninth Symphony is credited as his most performed work and loved world-wide because of the rousing chorus at the end, 'Ode to Joy'. The words for this 'ode' came from the poet Schiller but Beethoven himself added the line, 'all men are brothers'. This was truly visionary for his time when we remember that the background to Beethoven's life was one of European turmoil with the French Revolution and the Napoleonic wars. As a stirring symbol of freedom, it was Beethoven's Ninth that was played in celebration when the Berlin wall came down. Music lifts our spirits above the dark complexities of human behaviour.

Growing up in the sixties, I heard Bob Dylan and Joan Baez give voice to the anti-war movement. Their songs were haunting, the words of which I can still sing.

Every generation throws up a voice of protest and John the Baptist's rant, recorded in Matthew's gospel, is a classic protest song. We can be so preoccupied with the image of some desert weirdo in rough clothes eating (from our perspective) disgusting insects that we lose sight of the real man and his message. Remember, our Lord Jesus, John's cousin, called him the greatest of all prophets. This was a cherished son of the priest, Zechariah. As such John would have received formal education in the Law, the prophets and the wisdom literature of the Scriptures in the synagogue and the Temple. In the eyes of others' children, his was a privileged existence. He would have eaten better and dressed better than most. Everyone would have expected John to follow in his father's footsteps and become a priest.

However, the prophets (and there hadn't been prophets as such for about four hundred years) were men who proclaimed God's message by dramatic behaviour and living parables. So we see the son of respectable Zechariah and Elizabeth 'preaching in the desert'. This didn't mean he took himself off into obscurity, just that he removed himself from the position of comfort and privilege. Matthew emphasised this by the mention of camel's hair clothing (which was the clothing of the poor) and his peculiar diet, merely underlining John's reliance on God's providence. He chose the best position to guarantee an audience – the place where travellers stopped to rest and fill their water skins. The flowing river was ideal for the ritual washing and therefore for baptism to indicate public repentance and renewal. Let us not think of John as the wild man of the wilderness, but rather a Spirit-filled man of God (Luke 1:15).

And what was the message of this first century protest song?

A blast against complacency, dire threats of the consequence of living to please themselves and paying lip-service to God, and a revolutionary attitude to social compassion. To use contemporary terms, John spoke truth to power. He showed a better way, a way free from corruption, a way of sharing, a way of repentance. John repeated the message of the ancient prophets, the core tenets of living by the values of the kingdom of God. This is a message we need to voice today amidst all the corruption, greed and self-indulgence of the world's values. Most importantly of all, John pointed the people to Jesus.

Questions to consider

1. What do you consider is the worst problem in the world today?
2. In what ways could your lifestyle benefit others?

Verse

'On Jordan's bank the Baptist's cry announces that the Lord is nigh:
Awake and listen, for he brings glad tidings of the King of Kings.
So let us all our hearts prepare for Christ to come and enter there.'

John Chandler (1806–1876)

Prayer

Lord, I examine my life in the light of Your love. Help me to be aware of and to avoid hypocrisy, avarice and pride. Give me patience and compassion.

18 DEC

Opening prayer

Lord of all hopefulness, Lord of all joy,
May Your Holy Spirit open my eyes to the wonder of Your promise.
Still me, Lord, to receive Your blessing.

Bible verses

Isaiah 12:2–6
Romans 4:18–25

Ben was terrified. The caravan holiday was great fun, but each night a piercing noise made the little boy freeze and burst into tears. After four nights his father explained that it was only an owl, a beautiful bird, out looking for its supper. Gathered up in his father's arms, Ben looked towards the trees silhouetted against the night sky. Suddenly, an owl screeched, but this time there were no tears. Ben was happy and safe in his father's arms.

Great names in the Bible loom out across the years and we tend to take their faith for granted. From Abraham to the disciples, these faithful servants and witnesses to God stride across the pages of history. But if we take a cool, objective look at their circumstances, I don't think there was one of them who, at some point, had not been scared out of their wits. Some, like Moses, Gideon and Jeremiah, made plausible excuses why God should choose someone else.

At this time of year, when schools and churches perform nativity plays, we turn our minds to Joseph, Mary, the shepherds and the Magi. In first century Palestine we can be sure they all had good reason to be scared. Think about Joseph. After all, who wants their arranged marriage to turn into a scandal? Joseph is much underestimated and overlooked. His crucial choice to stand by Mary showed he was a man of honour and, above all, it proved how much he loved her (something that was by no means guaranteed in those days).

Think of the shepherds. The angel of the Lord tells them not to be afraid but Matthew recounts that they were 'terrified' (Luke 2:9)! The Magi, too, must have looked with fear at every cave opening and passing traveller, wondering if robbers would end their quest to find the new King. But maybe no one was in more turmoil than Mary. Matthew recounts that an angel appeared to Joseph and told him not to be afraid to take Mary as his wife: Luke's gospel records Mary's messenger as the angel Gabriel. Gabriel said to her also, 'Do not be afraid' (Luke 1:30). In those social circumstances that's a bit like preparing to walk a plank across Niagara Falls and someone saying, 'Don't worry'. All those serene portraits of Mary, draped in blue satin folds, have ingrained themselves into our subconscious, leaving the impression of a holy, obedient but one-dimensional girl.

Although no biblical characters were one-dimensional, we hardly ever give time to think about them as real people. We can take heart that God broke into the lives of men and women with genuine fears and doubts but in their obedience they found strength to trust. Their faith has proved inspirational through all time. God never failed them, neither will He fail us. They all lived prior to the crucifixion. Following the earth-shattering events of death and resurrection appearance, hundreds of people put their faith in Jesus, the Messiah (Acts 2:42).

Perhaps your faith has been deepened by someone who has shown faith in the face of great anguish. Rev Ian Coffey wrote about the death and resurrection of our Lord Jesus as, 'our source of hope and the foundation of our faith' (*Shock and Awe*, BRF, 2009 p27).

Questions to consider

1. How do you react when you are afraid?
2. Which biblical character's story or attitude do you find most helpful?

Verse

'Away with our fears, our sorrows and tears!
The glad morning draws near when our Saviour is born!'

Based on eighteenth century verse

Prayer

Lord, help me to trust and not be afraid. You are my strength and my salvation.

19 DEC

Opening prayer

Lord of all hopefulness, Lord of all joy,
May Your Holy Spirit open my eyes to the wonder of Your promises.
Centre me, Lord, into Your deep stillness.

Bible verses

Psalm 8
Colossians 1:15–23

The days are passing in a spin – Christmas will soon be here! Everyone seems to be going faster and faster, living their lives on skates! Why is it that as we approach any time of holiday, any opportunity to take a break from the routine treadmill, we fast-track a hundred more things to pack into a shorter space of time? Christmas is a time most people celebrate with time off work, and time for family and friends. Surely, God does not expect us to prepare for the birth of our Saviour with such frenetic activity that we end up too tired to think?

One way I love to relax is to wander out under a clear, night sky. It sounds pedestrian to put it like this but there is just so much up there! Even without a high-powered telescope, I'm lost in 'wonder, love and praise'. And when clouds obscure the millions of stars, I know they are still there. To gaze on the mysteries of space is enormously helpful in putting my life into perspective. I often quote King David, 'But who am I?' (1 Chron. 29:14) and, 'When I consider your heavens, the work of your fingers, the moon and the stars, which you have set in place, what is mankind ...?' (Psa. 8). The precision, intricacy and beauty of our universe are literally mind-blowing. If we studied it for our entire lives we would merely scratch the surface.

One beautiful, warm autumn evening in Galilee, our group of pilgrims gathered to pray beside the Sea of Galilee. Our mood music consisted of cicadas and the soft lapping of the water on the shingle; the tangible presence of the Lord Jesus wrapped us in silence. Our prayers ended but no one moved – all eyes looked up above the Syrian hills to the glorious full moon. The higher the moon rose, the more it reflected on the lake until there was a complete reflection right across the lake to where we stood. One member of the group said afterwards, 'It was like a silver pathway to heaven'. If we had stayed inside chatting over coffee, we would have missed an indelible spiritual experience, a precious moment filled with awe and hope.

Is your life too full to look up? Maybe God is asking you to step outside your usual routine – to lift your eyes away from a situation and be re-energised by the wonder of His sublime creation. Glimpse the moon in its cycles, the exquisite perfection of a petal, the sun sparkling on a river, the eyes of a child, the smile of a loved one – to glimpse these things lifts us out of ourselves. Small moments that make life worthwhile. Reminders of how small we are and how great our Creator.

My husband was a keen football supporter and, although not a fan myself, there was no escape from the Liverpool football club anthem *You'll Never Walk Alone*: such words of faith, written by the great American song-writer, Oscar Hammerstein II for a secular musical.

Let's walk on towards the celebration of our Saviour's birth, with hope in our hearts. Hope is a gift from Christ.

Questions to consider

1. When have you felt most alone?
2. Has there been a moment when you felt held in God's presence?

Verse

'For the beauty of each hour
Of the day and of the night,
Hill and vale and tree and flower,
Sun and moon and stars of light:
Gracious God to Thee we raise,
This our sacrifice of praise.'

Elliott Sandford Pierpoint (1835–1917)

Prayer

Christ beside me, Christ beneath me,
Christ around me, Christ above me.
Hold me in Your unfailing love.

20 DEC

Opening Prayer

Lord of all hopefulness, Lord of all joy,
May Your Holy Spirit open my eyes to the wonder of Your promises.
Still me, Lord, to receive Your blessing.

Bible verses

Psalm 130:5–8
Matthew 25:1–13

It had been a pleasant day with a pale sun tracking across a hazy blue sky. Just another day. Then, with bright, cheery smiles, the weather forecasters issued dire warnings. A great swathe of amber alerts dotted the country and, for some areas, even a patch of alerts in red. There was no excuse, everyone was told that significant snow falls were on the way and there would be disruption to all forms of transport. Weather forecasts have, on occasion, been known to lack accuracy in all aspects, but this particular forecast was correct almost to the minute. Television cameras projected pictures of abandoned vehicles, thousands of schools shut, airports closed and normal life was at a standstill. Mobile phone cameras showed children with toboggans and tin trays, frozen ponds and snow-dusted dogs. Hospital A & E departments amassed their winter toll of broken limbs while sensible people stayed indoors. People had been warned.

When reading the parable of the wise and foolish virgins, I can't help but have a sneaking sympathy for the girls who ran out of oil. I don't think I am alone when I say there have been times when I have found myself totally unprepared for a situation. But in these vivid, memorable and timeless stories, Jesus challenged His disciples, and challenges us, to face a deep truth. There was more to waiting for 'the bridegroom' to appear than just hanging around having a good time.

More than once Jesus said, 'Keep watch', most memorably in the Garden of Gethsemane (Mark 14:34). In closing his first letter to the Corinthian Christians, Paul urged: 'Be on your guard [keep watch], stand firm in the faith, be men of courage, be strong. Do everything in love' (1 Cor. 16:13–14). What a rousing sentence to encourage the new believers – and, surely, a solid text for every believer – for you and for me. As we go back into the wonderful book of Psalms we find the psalmist, too, had this need to be alert and wait for the Lord. 'My soul waits for the Lord more than watchmen wait for the morning' (Psa. 130:6). Here is the deep-rooted longing for the Lord to make Himself known. The hopes that had sustained the people through all their trials and tribulations were the hopes that found fulfilment in the person of Jesus.

In the picture language of Scripture, for instance in the Song of Songs and Isaiah, God is represented as the Bridegroom, and Jesus is the Bridegroom in Revelation chapter 22. These days, as parents know all too well, wedding preparations have become more and more elaborate in the quest to make the big day as perfect as possible.

This Advent season of 'waiting' and 'preparation' is our precious season to prepare ourselves spiritually not only to commemorate the Incarnation, but to acknowledge that we need to live in constant readiness and expectation of His coming again. To watch and pray. To be ready. How we need the power of the Holy Spirit to give us patience and perseverance for this life-long commitment.

Questions to consider

1. Would you say that you were ready for the coming of Jesus?
2. How would you put the parable of the wise and foolish virgins into a contemporary setting?

Verse

'O come, O come, Immanuel, release our captive souls
From worldly cares and self-indulgent goals:
O come, O Key of David, come, and lift our eyes above
To join the angel songs of love.

O come, O Day-spring, come, we wait your Advent here,
O come to us and drive away our fear.
Rejoice! Rejoice! Immanuel shall come to us,
Shall live in us for ever and for ever.'

Based on eighteenth century Latin Advent Antiphons

Prayer

Lord, help me to celebrate the gift of each day. Give me courage to watch and pray for your kingdom to come and give me the grace to do everything in love.

21 DEC

Opening prayer

Lord of all hopefulness, Lord of all joy,
May Your Holy Spirit open my eyes to the wonder of Your promises.
Still me, Lord, to receive Your blessing.

Bible verses

1 Chronicles 16:23–31
Psalm 72:1–4,15–20

You'll not find a more enthusiastic royalist than Vera. She is one of those ardent fans who, over the years, has camped overnight on London's pavements to secure a front row seat for the passing pageantry. The love affair with royalty has very ancient origins as individuals and nations seem always to have craved role models. In the UK coronation service the shout goes up: 'God save the Queen!' a shout that has its origins in the mists of time!

From the Chronicler we glimpse an exuberant song of thanksgiving from the great King David, the king whose reign was more a theocracy. And from the psalmist we have the heritage of this 'royal' psalm (Psa. 72), which may even have been used at the enthronement of King Solomon. Over the years it was also used as a hymn of praise to Israel's God. The God of Israel was the Lord God of Hosts, the exalted Sovereign Lord of all, before whom all people, even the king, bowed in worship. But after Solomon, with few exceptions, kings left a lot to be desired, to say the least – their lives dismissed to history's scrap-heap with curt condemnation, '... they did evil in the eyes of the LORD' (Judg. 3:12).

However, the nation persisted in its desire for a king and the Messianic overtones, the unquenchable hope for the kingdom of the Lord, gathered momentum with each new reign: the worse the king, the greater the longing for the reign of God's Messiah. We tend to narrow our view of David to a few stories of his dramatic exploits; the vivid account of the young David killing the massive Goliath; his tense escapes from King Saul and his underhand conniving to take another man's wife. David is, in fact, one of the best recorded of the Old Testament characters; we have a warts-and-all account of his life but also insights into the depth of his faith. At times he dipped, but don't we all!

The book of Chronicles includes several gems, including the verses for today. It's quite amazing to think that when these words were first recorded, their world was flat and focused on the relatively small area we call the Middle East and the Mediterranean. However, as Christmas approaches, those far off dreams have come true as people all over the world sing hymns and songs rejoicing in the birth of our Saviour and King.

My mind goes to those awesome words from the book of Revelation, 'The kingdom of the world has become the kingdom of our Lord and of his Messiah, and he will reign for ever and ever' Rev. 11:15). This, of course, is the very same idea as the kingdom of God of which Jesus spoke: 'The kingdom of God has come near' (Mark 1:15). What signs of this kingdom have you seen?

Questions to consider

1. If you have been to a royal event, to what lengths did you go to prepare for the occasion?
2. Why has the coronation of a Queen or King usually been in a Cathedral?

Verse

'Kingdom of Christ, for Thy coming we pray:
Hasten, O Father, the dawn of the day
When this new song Thy creation shall sing
Satan is vanquished and Jesus is King.
Come let us sing: Praise to our King,
Jesus our King, Jesus our King ...'

Charles Silvester Horne (1865–1914)

Prayer

Lord, I pray: Your kingdom come, Your will be done on earth as it is in heaven.

Suggestions for group study for Week 3

Preparation

Light the third candle on an Advent wreath and play a song or piece of instrumental music to focus the group.

Focus

Choose a day from the week and say the opening prayer. Then consider the Bible readings, inviting as many people as possible to read. Refer to the input and questions.

Discussion point

I am a firm believer that we should look up more. Many years ago, I drove my uncle from Essex to Cornwall. He thoroughly enjoyed himself glued to the map on his knees, busy telling me when to expect dual carriageways and roundabouts and which town or village we were passing. I tried to lift his attention to a bird of prey, fields of ripening corn and distant cloud formations, but he resolutely kept his eyes on the map.
How can we look up more?

Prayer

Lord of the universe, we would look up and away from ourselves to see Your glory in the face of Christ.

Conclude by saying the Lord's Prayer and sharing either the Grace or the Peace.

WEEK 4

New Birth into a Living Hope

Allegro! The tempo accelerates towards the birth, the climax of Advent being the arrival (advent) of the Saviour of the World. From that moment history changed. Jesus radiates the compassionate, inclusive love which gives life to peace and hope for all people: 'Our God contracted to a span, incomprehensibly made man' (Charles Wesley).

22 DEC

Opening prayer

Awaken me, Lord.
Into the familiarity of the nativity story
Breathe the freshness of Your Holy Spirit.

Bible verse

Amos 5:21–24
Matthew 23:23–26

2012 was the greatest year in the history of the world! This was the bold statement in a newspaper article last December which claimed, 'never in the history of the world has there been less hunger, less disease and more prosperity' (*The Spectator*, 15 December 2012). If this is true then we have every reason to thank God for the tireless efforts of those working on the United Nations Millennium Development Goals. However, we cannot close our eyes to the continuation of war, violence, oppression and degradation that mar the image of Christ in our brothers and sisters, not only across the world but in our own areas. The levels of poverty and inequality cast a shadow on all the Christmas celebrations. Celebrations are good and necessary – they lift our spirits – but the message of the Incarnation carries responsibility. We must never lose sight of those in need.

The prophets spoke out in the name of the Lord God; they railed against complacency as well as inequality. Jesus said, 'the poor you will always have with you' (Matt. 26:11), therefore we need to be constantly aware that the multitude of social problems do not fade conveniently into oblivion during the season of Christmas. Advent is our time for taking stock of spiritual balances. Do we cherry-pick the Word of God so long as it chimes with our comfort zone?

Seven hundred and fifty years before the birth of Jesus, Amos, a wise and godly shepherd, was not a happy bunny. The fact that he tended sheep out on the Judean hills did not mean he was unaware of what was going on in the towns and cities in the lives of the affluent and influential. Nights under the stars gave him time to think, to pray, to weigh up the consequences of the nation's self-indulgence and complacency. Illegal and immoral slavery, over-taxation and land-grabbing, oppression and injustice hid behind a religious facade. Amos heard the mind of God in his heart. The people's prosperity had gone to their heads, religion became distorted to their own advantage and they worshipped themselves in the short-sighted, hedonistic way of every acquisitive culture. Imagine Amos sheltering from a violent storm, and in the deep cracks of thunder raging from the clouds, the Word of the Lord throbs in his heart. He leaves his sheep with the other shepherds (Amos 1:1 tells us he was 'one of the shepherds') to begin life as God's prophet. The uncompromising message he proclaimed was one of the most direct, urgent and strident. But, and here comes that loaded three letter word, *but* – where else do we find a correspondingly strident tone? In Matthew chapter 23, our Lord lambasts the Pharisees and teachers of the Law. If you have time to read the whole chapter you will see why the teachers of the Law, the Pharisees and Sadducees would have been incandescent at such public humiliation from an itinerant preacher.

It's tempting to ask, 'What's new?' and we should ask this question because we have an answer. Peter, the great disciple turned evangelist, along with Christians scattered throughout Asia Minor, faced severe persecution. Knowing he was likely to be killed for his faith, he delivered the most important message to encourage the believers: God 'has given us [you and me] new birth into a living hope through ... Jesus Christ' (1 Pet.1:3). Praise God!

Questions to consider

1. How can I translate 'new birth' into 'new lifestyle'?
2. Where is prophecy evident today?

Verse

'Jesus calls us from the worship
Of the vain world's golden store,
From each idol that would keep us,
Saying, "Christian, love me more."'

C.F. Alexander (1818–1895)

Prayer

Lord, help me to serve You in simple, loving trust.

23 DEC

Opening prayer

Awaken me, Lord.
Into the familiarity of the nativity story
Breathe the freshness of Your Holy Spirit.

Bible verses

Matthew 1:1–17
1 John 2:28–29, 3:1–3

We've all got one. We may not have done anything about it, but thousands of people have become addicted to researching their family tree. Genealogy has leapt from the confines of minority hobby into the realms of popular entertainment to become international big business. Fascination with our family trees has never been so enthralling, unless that is, we think back to biblical times! Matthew, writing for a Jewish audience, rattles off this long list of ancestors to prove that Jesus, his Lord and Master, is not only descended from both the father of the nation, Abraham, but also their iconic king, David – credentials so impressive they gave immediate authority to Jesus. We cannot over-estimate the importance to the biblical mind of family ties, and though we may be tempted to skip these verses to concentrate on the birth narrative, for Matthew and his contemporaries, this family tree was a vital foundation in understanding who Jesus was.

Did you notice that within the list of worthy patriarchs, this roll of honour, there were five women? To mention women was unusual enough, but to name them was extraordinary, especially when we consider what the Bible tells us about four of them. Let's look at the first four. Tamar was abused by her father-in-law; Rahab was known as a prostitute, Ruth came from the land of Moab; and Uriah's wife, Bathsheba, may or may not have been complicit in her adultery with King David (2 Sam. 11:2–5). The fifth is Mary, the mother of Jesus 'who is called the Messiah' (Matt. 27:22). Every family tree has its surprises and shadowy figures and apart from Mary and Ruth, the other three were tinged with scandal. Even Ruth came from a despised nation. This is no ordinary family tree. These are the ancestors of Jesus our Lord – God appearing in human flesh with the DNA of three unlikely women – Ruth the gentile from another country, and Rahab and Bathsheba of dubious backgrounds!

So if that was the Jesus' family tree, where do we come in? The pastoral letter of John to congregations in general assures believers that 'we are children of God' (1 John 3:2) and again, 'Everyone who believes that Jesus is the Christ is born of God' (1 John 5:1). That brings every believer in Jesus Christ into the same family and that, miraculously, includes you and me. There is no mistake: John is waiting for Jesus to return (compare Acts 1:11). Therefore, all His followers, all His family must live according to His teaching of compassion and righteousness. As well as the 'letter of love', John's letter has been termed 'the wisdom epistle', highlighting once more the importance to the biblical mind of wisdom. John was an old man when he wrote his letters, but they resonate with the clarity of the eye-witness to Jesus that he was (1 John 1:1). His message is sprinkled with familiar words of contrast, love/hate, light/darkness, old/new, life/death, truth/falsehood.

There is a hymn which begins: 'It is a thing most wonderful, almost too wonderful to be' (W.W. How). That's how I would describe the blessing of being a child of God.

Questions to consider

1. How would you describe being 'a child of God'?
2. Jesus Christ will come again. How do we prepare for Him?

Verse

'Wisdom unsearchable,
God the invisible,
Love indestructible
In frailty appears.
Lord of infinity,
Stooping so tenderly,
Lifts our humanity
To the heights of His throne.
O what a mystery,
Meekness and majesty.
Bow down and worship
For this is your God.'

Graham Kendrick

Prayer

Lord, I give You my praise and thanksgiving that I belong to Your family through Jesus Christ. Thank You for the faith, hope and love by which Christians encourage each other in Your worldwide family.

24 DEC

Opening prayer

Awaken me, Lord.
Into the familiarity of the nativity story
Breathe the freshness of Your Holy Spirit.

Bible verses

Luke 1:46–55

Right at the beginning of his gospel, the Gentile doctor, Luke, explains that his information has been gathered from those 'who from the first were eye-witnesses' (Luke 1:2). And the most important eye-witness, the only one who was at the beginning and at the end of Jesus' earthly life, was His mother, Mary. Therefore, it's a fair assumption that Mary was the direct source of much of the material in Luke's gospel. How amazing that we can share the thoughts and recollections of this unique and unassuming woman.

Full of hopes and dreams, Mary took herself off to visit her cousin Elizabeth, 'and hurried to a town in the hill country of Judea' (Luke 1:39). Traditionally this is Ein Kerem, a delightful place beloved of artists, on the outskirts of Jerusalem, within walking distance for Zechariah to attend at the Temple.

Education in biblical times was for boys, while girls were taught all the home skills by their mothers. However, Mary's beautiful song of praise shows how much attention she had paid in the synagogue, for it is liberally sprinkled with references to God's covenant promise to Abraham, to Hannah's prayer and to the Psalms: a remarkable song rooted in scriptural aspirations. Delia Smith, in her book *Feast for Advent*, wrote: 'Scripture is a deep well of information and inspiration that never runs dry.' That is the mystery and miracle of the inspired Word of God. Mary must have been a deeply spiritual and intelligent girl. Joy and praise gush through her words, telling the world, in today's words, 'I'm the luckiest girl in the world'.

The great God, the Saviour of all the despised, oppressed and disregarded, this same God had kept the ancient promises; her child would be '... great and will be called the Son of the Most High. The Lord God will give him the throne of his father David ... his kingdom will never end' (Luke 1:32–33). Glory hallelujah! What a vision of Utopia and a hope that was to be realised. This would be the new world, the new government, the kingdom of God. Expectations in ecstatic overdrive!

Even in the last century, with so many countries emerging from colonial rule, this Magnificat, as Mary's song is called, was earnestly discouraged because it was considered to be a 'revolutionary canticle'. That's hard to understand from our standpoint of freedom. But the Jews of Jesus' time were not free and revolution is always the desperate search for renewal. The idea that 'he [God] has sent the rich away empty' (Luke 1:53), to a foreign, ruling power, was, at the very least, dangerous. But then, the kingdom of God is an upside down, renewed world, the reverse of our power-hungry, acquisitive and self-centred culture. Just think about Jesus' teaching in the Sermon on the Mount (Matt. 5–7).

Motherhood for Mary would bring the greatest joy in watching her son mature: immeasurable pride in His miracles and teaching, but also cruel hurt and rejection when her son seemed to prefer the company of strangers to that of His own family. Then she was to endure the most terrible moment for any mother, the total helplessness of watching her son die. But that was not the end. Mary stayed with the disciples as they gathered in the upper room (Acts 1:14) and it is almost certain that Mary was present for the coming of the Holy Spirit at Pentecost. This was a rollercoaster of emotion and experience she shared with her confidant, Luke.

Questions to consider

1. Would you consider that the Magnificat has lost its resonance for our affluent nations?
2. What characteristics of Mary catch your imagination?

Verse

'We are waiting, Holy Jesus, all is ready for your birth.
We've prepared our Beth'lem manger,
The lowly manger of our hearts.
Come now, Jesus, we will love You,
Bring your Love-light to this earth.'

Prayer

Loving God, this night tingles with expectation. Fill me with awe and wonder. Open my heart to hope and renewal.

25 DEC

Opening prayer

Awaken me, Lord.
Into the familiarity of the nativity story
Breathe the freshness of Your Holy Spirit.

Bible verses

Luke 2:4–7
Galatians 4:4–5

The day of Jesus' birth – 'O come, let us adore him'. In his last sermon as Archbishop of Canterbury, Dr Rowan Williams concluded by saying, 'That adoration, that wondering gaze at the child in the manger, is where faith is born; and where faith is born so is the new world of Jesus and His Spirit'.

This is a day so crammed with busyness and fraught with things to remember that we can be completely submerged by extraneous Christmas wrappings. Greeting people, singing carols, eating and celebrating, opening presents, eating, contacting those we love by Skype, phone and text, eating and clearing up! Or maybe your Christmas Day is far from what you had hoped for, the whole festive fling petering out in anticlimax leaving you feeling lost and adrift from other people's joy.

The build up to Christmas Day has been a long time coming. Some shops can't even wait until September to entice customers to prepare, buy and store away for 25 December. The 'golden oldies' ring out from radios, throughout stores and groups of carol singers and Salvation Army bands serenade us in arcades and on street corners. During these weeks, millions of pounds are raised for excellent and worthy causes and children eagerly cross off the days on their Advent calendars ... all eyes strain forward to Christmas Day. Now it is here.

For a brief moment let's pare away the frippery and glimpse God's stupendous gift: the mystery of life, the continuing miracle of faith and hope. Pause to gaze in wonder, love and praise. Matthew's version is hardly two lines: '... she gave birth to a son. And he [Joseph] gave him the name Jesus' (Matt 1:25). Luke's version is equally succinct, taking one verse to record the Saviour's birth: 'While they were there [Bethlehem], the time came for the baby to be born, and she gave birth to her firstborn, a son. She wrapped him in cloths and placed him in a manger ...' (Luke 2:6–7).

The birth. A sacred miracle. New life. The greatest wonder in the world. The focus of this day is the birth of Jesus Christ our Lord, a baby lying in the hay: a vulnerable baby wrapped up and put out of harm's way in a feeding trough. What a remarkable cradle for the one who would say, 'I am the bread of life' (John 6:35).

A few years ago I came across a quotation which ran like this: 'We can be so busy adoring the baby we forget to worship the Christ who offers us eternal life'. If ever we were in danger of doing that, the apostle Paul puts his own slant on the birth and the reason for the incarnation. God's own Son came into our world, born as we are and into human circumstances to heal the breach between heaven and earth. Do you find it interesting that the first people to communicate the message of Jesus Christ were far more concerned with the impact of His death and resurrection?

Gaze and wonder

1. How will this day be different from any other?
2. What special moment of Christmas would you like to share?

Verse

'Yea. Lord, we greet Thee, born this happy morning,
Jesus, to thee be glory given.
Word of the Father, now in flesh appearing:
O come let us adore him, Christ the Lord.'

Eighteenth century

Prayer

Our Lord and our God, we come as the visitors to the stable long ago. We bring the gold of our love, the frankincense of our intercessions and the myrrh of our bitter sorrows. Let Your light so kindle our faith that all those whose lives touch ours this day may find their gloom dispelled and their faith renewed. Let the joy of new birth radiate this day and our whole lives.

Lesley Weatherhead (adapted)

26 DEC

Opening Prayer

Awaken me, Lord.
Into the familiarity of the nativity story
Breathe the freshness of Your Holy Spirit.

Bible verses

Luke 2:8–20

I have cleaned out pigsties, fed chickens and milked cows but I've not kept sheep. I would have loved to keep sheep and most likely would have become a life-long vegetarian. I remember being with a group on a pilgrim coach as it rumbled along the dusty road into Bethlehem. Suddenly a small flock of lop-eared sheep overflowed down a broken bank and stood in the middle of the road. Quick as a flash, two young boys, present day shepherds, led their animals along the road and back to where they belonged. It all took several minutes, in which time, every pilgrim's camera had captured this enchanting biblical scene. A peaceful, pastoral sight, a balm after the concrete separation wall through which we had entered Bethlehem, this city of David and birth place of our Lord. We gave thanks for this unexpected gift of revelation; we had witnessed a timeless cameo; one that Jesus would have seen daily.

One late afternoon, when I lived near Epping Forest, I was walking with friends, engaged in lively, and perhaps loud, conversation. We rounded a bend in the pathway only to be met by another group who began to wave at us to be quiet! Our merry chatter dried up in an instant under their disapproving scowls. As we crept near the leader whispered an explanation. Nightingales were being re-introduced to that area and the group was checking up on the success of the venture. We stood and listened. Peering up into the thick canopy of leaves, we heard it: the pure song of a nightingale. Left to our own noisy and enjoyable stomp through the forest, we would never have heard that beautiful song. It is a precious memory now that I no longer visit Epping Forest and I feel privileged to have heard a nightingale sing.

It's interesting to ponder on the song of the angels. The shepherds were in the right place at the right time. Their ears were tuned to listen for sounds of danger. They could recognise a sheep in distress or a friend approaching, but angels? This must have been an experience they talked about for the rest of their lives. But, maybe that is not the important lesson for us. Is it that God is saying to us, 'Sometimes you need to stop, to be quiet, to listen to My voice. Then you will see My glory, then you will understand that every soul is of equal importance to Me. Listen and respond to my love'.

The New Zealand writer Joy Cowley wrote: 'Once more comes the music, angel song that lifts our hearts and tunes our ears to the harmony of the universe' ('Nativity' from *Aotearoa Psalms*).

The American author Larry Libby wrote: 'Late on a sleepy,

star-spangled night, those angels peeled back the sky, just like you would tear open a sparkling Christmas present. Then, with joy pouring out of heaven like water through a broken dam, they began to shout and sing the message that baby Jesus had been born. The world had a Saviour! The angels called it "Good News" and it was.'

So may we tune our ears and respond to the angels' song: 'Glory to God in the highest heaven, and on earth peace to those on whom his favour rests' (Luke 2:14).

Questions to consider

1. Whom would you define as the 'shepherds' of the twenty-first century?
2. In what ways will you give time to hear the angels' song?

Verse

'Shepherds in the field abiding, watching o'er your flocks by night,
God with us is now residing, yonder shines the infant Light:
Come and worship, Christ the new-born King.'

James Montgomery (1771–1854)

Prayer

Lord God, may the message of the angels fill my heart with hope and joy and give me courage to share good news with those who have celebrated Christmas without Christ.

27 DEC

Opening Prayer

Awaken me, Lord.
Into the familiarity of the nativity story
Breathe the freshness of Your Holy Spirit.

Bible verses

Isaiah 49:1–4,7
Matthew 2:1–12

The nativity characters were dressed up at the back of the church. Joseph proudly sported authentic headgear from Nazareth, shepherds grumbled over who was to hold the toy lamb and two small angels vied over silver tinsel. In the corner lay the nine-week-old baby who would star in the manger. The clock ticked towards the appointed start of the service. Furrowed brows – the third king had not arrived and, more worryingly, nor had Mary. Anyone who has had first-hand experience of such services knows the stress of last minute pitfalls, but often they bring out unexpected joys. A larger angel morphed swiftly into Mary without shedding her tinsel and one of the mothers stood in for the third king. Sighs of relief. The nativity proceeded like clockwork.

In eleventh century France, they performed a pageant, *The Office of the Star,* and a record exists of a nativity play performed in Rome in the twelfth century. However, it is more than probable that enactments of biblical stories were performed many centuries before. From the ancient camp fires to the current renaissance of block-buster films, young and old love a good story. And what a good God story this is! Quoting from Joy Cowley again: 'And here again is the star, that white flame of truth, blazing the way for us through a desert of tired words'.

Our only reference to the eastern strangers making their way to Bethlehem comes from Matthew's gospel. He only called them Magi, wise people, (the word is not gender specific) but whoever they were and wherever they came from, they risked everything to find the object of their hopes and dreams. Probably they have been given the title of Kings because of the Old Testament prophecies that kings and princes 'will see you', which underlined the belief that when the Messiah arrived, He would have greater authority than any earthly king or ruler.

We saw on 6 December how the biblical writers elevated wisdom, and again, in Matthew's gospel, we see that even wisdom bows before the child. Behind this visual pageant lies the truth that Jesus Christ, the Messiah, has come for all nations. The wise ones from the east gathered up their precious gifts and began a journey with an unknown destination. They looked into the face of a child and registered a new life in whom all nations could unite in peace. And Matthew tells us that these wise people returned to their homes a different way. Herod's duplicitous request to know where this child could be found was warning enough. The Magi had met his sort before.

But I like to think that those holy foreigners returned to their homes changed people; from the experience of their pilgrimage they would never be the same again. And I would like to think that we too can be changed as we gaze at the Christ-child. As we cut through our own desert of tired words, let us worship and adore the Son of God with our gifts of time, compassion and trust. Let us nurture hope in our hearts that wherever the journey of life takes us, our final destination will be with Christ in glory.

Questions to consider

1. Think about a time in your life when your journey led you to an unexpected place.
2. What gifts would you like to offer to Jesus Christ? What have you offered?

Verse

'Look up! Look East to where the sun rises –
Look for the glory of the Son.
Star, whose crisp, bright Light penetrates the world's dark ink of sky
And, laser light across the worlds
Shines the beam of hope for every searching heart.
Look up! There shines the bright and Morning Star!
Awake from sleep and follow ... follow ... follow.'

Prayer

Lord, help me to follow my dreams. Open my eyes to the contribution and value of all who seek to serve humanity in the name of the Prince of Peace.

28 DEC

Opening prayer

Awaken me, Lord.
Into the familiarity of the nativity story
Breathe the freshness of Your Holy Spirit.

Bible verses

Luke 2:25–35
Psalm 37:7–9

Recently, making a list of fifty things to do before you die has become a popular pastime. What a wild variation of hopes and dreams get listed on these fantasy lists: swimming with dolphins, witnessing the Aurora Borealis, finding a Roman coin or holding a first grandchild. I wonder what would feature high on your list of fifty must-do things? On my list is the hope that I might get a chance to be an extra with a two second walk-on part in some lavish, period film!

Lists apart, in these days of medical miracles, healthier food and all-round living conditions, we don't like to think, or talk, about dying. When people fall ill, we expect the doctors to make them well again and as each decade arrives we kid ourselves that we are as young as we feel and cling to every comforting cliché we can think of. But only a few generations ago, longevity was not regarded as a right. Foul diseases made death in the family or in the same street relatively common. People could not escape their own mortality.

Luke doesn't specifically say Simeon was an old man, and he may not have been as old as tradition has accepted. What we do know is that after taking the forty-day-old baby Jesus in his arms, he felt he could die content. If you like, Simeon had a two-second walk-on part in this epic period drama. On one level the only thing we know about him is his name. But, as the Irish comedian Frank Carson used to say, '... there's more'. We know Simeon was devout and righteous, a thoroughly good man, steeped in Scripture and waiting for God's Messiah, and 'the Holy Spirit was on him' (Luke 2:25). This is a very significant mention. Sometimes we pigeon-hole the Holy Spirit into Pentecost after the death and resurrection of our Lord, but Luke's gospel put great emphasis on the Holy Spirit right from the promise to Zechariah that his son would be 'filled with the Holy Spirit' (Luke 1:15). The Holy Spirit was at the conception of Jesus (Luke 1:35), Mary's cousin Elizabeth was filled with the Holy Spirit (Luke 1:41) and Zechariah was filled with the Holy Spirit as he prophesied (Luke 1:67ff). Luke's writing makes it crystal clear that the Holy Spirit is integral to all God's actions. This was no new thought, for every devout Jew knew that the Spirit of God was present at the birth of creation (Gen. 1:2).

Although Luke was a Gentile, he used the typical rabbinical method of threefold repetition to stress a vital point. In this cameo of Jesus' presentation in the Temple, the seat of the Most High God, Luke adds two more references to the Holy Spirit in Simeon's life. The Holy Spirit 'revealed' to him that God's kingdom was close. Things Simeon had spent his life hoping for were about to be fulfilled. The prayers of his devout life were about to be answered. Secondly, the Holy Spirit nudged Simeon to go to the Temple, outside his routine, to be in the place God needed him to be.

Let's remember the Holy Spirit is not confined to the pages of the Bible, but is just as vital and integral to our own lives as to those about whom we have read.

Questions to consider

1. What do you think of Simeon's words to Mary?
2. Simeon was devout and righteous. By what words would you like to be remembered?

Verse

'Like Mary, let us ponder in our mind
God's wondrous love in saving lost mankind.
Saved by his love, incessant we shall sing,
Eternal praise to heaven's almighty King.'

John Byrom (1692–1763)

Prayer

Lord, there is so much to think about. I pray for wisdom and discernment.

Suggestions for group study for Week 4

Preparation

Light the fourth candle on an Advent wreath and play a song or piece of instrumental music to focus the group. As this is the final group study, you might like to spend some time considering 31 December in detail.

Prayer

God of our past, our present and our future, we commit ourselves, and those we love, into Your eternal keeping.

Conclude by saying the Lord's Prayer and sharing either the Grace or the Peace.

A Future and a Hope

Joy to the world the Lord is come! In this symphony of faith, there is no finale. As we reprise the themes of our Advent journey we know that the rhythms of life that lie ahead will include the minuets and fugues, the scherzos and requiems through which every human life draws ever closer to God. May we stride into the future in tune with our heavenly conductor's beat, confident in the eternal music of the soul.

29 DEC

Opening prayer

I come to You,
Lord of my past, my present and my future.
I commit myself, and those I love, into Your eternal keeping.

Bible verses

Jeremiah 29:11–13
Hebrews 6:13–20

What possible similarities can there be between the despondent exiles in Babylon, first and second generation Christians and ourselves? Well, in 2500 years human nature does not change – we all ask unanswerable questions.

The mood of the exiles is captured in the words of Psalm 137: 'By the rivers of Babylon we sat and wept when we remembered Zion' (v.1). Their morale had reached rock bottom and they wondered what had happened to their God. There are few emotions so debilitating as that of feeling rejected by the person in whom you have placed all your hopes. We can imagine them sifting through all the promises the prophets had uttered in the name of the Lord God ... what had become of those promises? Their future looked hopeless.

After the initial enthusiasm from the Christian converts, the group of believers to whom the letter to the Hebrews was addressed were having a bit of a spiritual wobble. They were on the receiving end of growing persecution from both their fellow Jews and the Roman authorities. It is impossible for us to adequately understand the predicament of those who risked not only their own lives, but also the lives of loved ones.

Christians in Europe are a shrinking remnant. Christians in certain parts of Africa have become victims of violent persecution and even death. There are many countries where it can be dangerous to be a follower of Jesus Christ. People say, 'Why does your God allow this or that catastrophe? Such and such person does not deserve to suffer', etc. We may have times of personal panic when God seems out of reach and doubts cascade through our minds.

Past generations have asked the same questions; fought with the same doubts. Satan is the ultimate deceiver and never gives up. I believe God is speaking to us through the words of Scripture, 'Take heart, I am with you, don't give up'. It is as though we are listening to the prophet Jeremiah as he urges us to realise that all is not lost, there is a future and a hope! It is up to us to turn to God, earnestly and sincerely, and we will find He is always present. If we were to shred the thirteen chapters of Hebrews down to a couple of sentences, it would be something like: 'God is faithful, Jesus Christ has greater authority than Moses and any of the prophets or angels. Hang in there, for God's promises are true'.

My personal favourite phrase from this letter is: 'We have this hope as an anchor for the soul' (Heb. 6:19). Those words evoke such strength and encouragement and I believe at the cusp of a new year we all need strength and encouragement whatever our circumstances, for none of us knows what lies ahead. My prayer is that we may be confident in knowing the loving Lord who holds our future in His eternity.

Questions to consider

1. What is your anchor?
2. God is with you all the way – how does that change things?

Verse

'Will your anchor hold in the storms of life
When the clouds unfold their wings of strife?
When the strong tides lift, and the cables strain,
Will your anchor drift, or firm remain?
We have an anchor ... fastened to the Rock which cannot move,
Grounded firm and deep in the Saviour's love.'

Priscilla Jane Owens (1829–1907)

Prayer

God be in my head and in my understanding,
God be in my eyes and in my looking,
God be in my mouth and in my speaking,
God be in my heart and in my thinking,
God be at my end and my departing.

Fifteenth century

30 DEC

Opening prayer

I come to You,
Lord of my past, my present and my future,
I commit myself, and those I love, into Your eternal keeping.

Bible verses

John 12:12–16
Philippians 2:1–11

Two expressions of Jesus as Son of God and Messiah. Two glimpses of how the people of His time responded to what they saw and heard. A reminder that Jesus was viewed through the lens of prophecy and expectation.

The apostle Paul dictated most of his letters to explain to new believers the life, death and resurrection of the Lord Jesus. When you think that the recipients of his letters had never seen the Lord, and lived hundreds of miles from where Jesus spent His earthly ministry, we catch a glimpse of the urgency and the seriousness of Paul's writing. This Pharisee and persecutor of converts to Christianity was transformed by his meeting with the risen Christ on the road to Damascus (Acts 9). Paul spent the rest of his life communicating the great miracle of God's redeeming love in Jesus and encouraging everyone, Jew and Gentile alike, to give their hearts to the Saviour (Rom. 1:1–6). Sadly, he had to address quarrelling factions, misunderstandings and false beliefs. Such is our human frailty.

Paul was the archetypal author of well argued prose, so where did this glorious song of faith in Philippians 2 come from? It is thought to be one of the earliest Christian hymns, or creeds, used by members of the growing number of congregations. This is not only prize-winning poetry; it forms the very basis of our faith. Everything is here: the divinity of Jesus (v6), the incarnation (v7), crucifixion (v8), resurrection (v9) and final triumph (vv10–11).

All this inspired poetry also contains a direct challenge to every believer, including you and me. Every follower of Jesus Christ must set aside their own agenda and learn, in love, the attributes of discipleship – humility and obedience. We have no rights but the solemn responsibility to live as Jesus taught. We witness to Him by our willingness to follow His teaching, the way of justice and peace, and in our compassionate service to others.

Philippi was a vibrant city and Paul's message drew converts from every area of life. From Luke's account in Acts 16 we know that the first Christians in Philippi included Lydia, a wealthy merchant, as well as a slave girl and a world-weary jailor. The compelling message of Jesus Christ cut across gender, race and culture, just as it does today.

William Dunkerley was a successful businessman. Born in 1852, he lived his long life with the background of international aggression and tragedy: the Crimean War, the Boer wars, the First World War and the rise of fascism. He died during the Second World War. Nevertheless, he had great faith that Jesus Christ offered a better way, a rebirth into new life and therefore, a renewed hope. He was a prolific writer who left this poem:

> 'In Christ there is no East or West,
> In him no South or North,
> But one great fellowship of love
> Throughout the whole wide earth.'
>
> William Dunkerley (1852–1941)

Questions to consider

1. Consider the proverb: 'A leopard cannot change its spots' in relation to the apostle Paul.
2. How would you describe Christianity to someone who had never heard of Jesus?

Verse

'Kings shall fall down before him,
And gold and incense bring;
All nations shall adore him,
His praise all people sing.
To him shall prayer unceasing
And daily vows ascend,
His kingdom still increasing,
His kingdom without end.'

James Montgomery (1771–1854) based on Psalm 72

Prayer

May the grace of our Lord Jesus Christ, the Love of God and the fellowship of the Holy Spirit be my guide and my goal in the coming year.

31 DEC

Opening prayer

I come to You,
Lord of my past, my present and my future.
I commit myself, and those I love, to Your eternal keeping.

Bible verses

Joshua 1:9–10
Romans 15:5–13

Have we reached the end or the beginning? In the busy shipping lanes where the English Channel opens into the Atlantic Ocean, the rugged end of Cornwall, Land's End, is literally the end of land, the last sight of England. However, passengers in ships coming in the opposite direction look on the exact same outcrop of Land's End as the beginning of England.

We are all travelling at different stages along our life's journey, and whether we are holding on to this year or impatient to begin a new year, let us pause to celebrate hope. It has been this timeless attitude that has enabled God's people to trust in Him, to look beyond themselves and strive for a better world.

Joshua's mentor and life-long leader, Moses, was dead and Joshua was about to lead God's people into the promised land. What an awesome responsibility. Look again at what God says to him: 'The LORD your God will be with you wherever you go' (Josh. 1:9). Does that remind you of another promise? Jesus, the Word made flesh, made a final and momentous promise to His disciples on that mountain in Galilee: 'And surely I am with you always, to the very end of the age' (Matt. 28:20).

The verses we are looking at today, which the apostle Paul wrote to the congregation in Rome, reach out to us as a précis of our Advent thoughts. He offers encouragement to all who seek to follow our Lord and Saviour Jesus Christ, and stresses that Jesus came to this world to fulfil God's promises to Abraham and those made through the prophets. Paul refers to Isaiah to underline that Jesus was the true successor to King David, the promised Messiah. Our passage ends with verse 13 which, to me, is one of the most heart-felt blessings in the Bible. What do the words mean to you as you step into an unknown New Year? You may have heavy responsibilities in front of you; you may be stepping out on your own for the first time. God says, 'Do not fear, for I am with you' (Isa. 41:10).

Let me share an idea that has helped me over the past few years. The most beautiful music in the world is merely a jumble of silent squiggles on the paper until a musician transforms the squiggles into the sounds we are meant to hear. And so it is with our faith. Christianity is silent and powerless unless the followers of Jesus Christ visibly and audibly *live* the harmony of God's kingdom for the world to see and hear.

Whatever our experience through this Advent and Christmas season, let us hold on and have faith that our hope begins and ends in God, the source of all hope.

Questions to consider

1. Tennyson wrote, 'Hope smiles from the threshold of the year to come ...' What are your hopes for the New Year?
2. How do you plan to continue your journey with Jesus?

Verse

'Teach me to dance to the beat of your heart,
Teach me to move in the power of your Spirit,
Teach me to walk in the light of your presence,
Teach me to dance to the beat of your heart.

Teach me to love with your heart of compassion,
Teach me to trust in the word of your promise,
Teach me to hope in the day of your coming,
Teach me to dance to the beat of your heart.'

Graham Kendrick

Prayer

Dear Lord, all that I am, all that I have, all that through Your grace I may become, I commit to You in the heartbeat of hope.